Come Like Shadows

Come Like Shadows

Welwyn Wilton Katz

COTEAU BOOKS
TWENTY-FIVE YEARS

Cover and interior illustration by Martin Springett.
Cover and book design by Duncan Campbell.

Printed and bound in Canada at Transcontinental Printing.

First published by Penguin Books Canada Limited, 1993.

Canadian Cataloguing in Publication Data

Katz, Welwyn.
Come like shadows
ISBN 1-55050-170-4

1. Macbeth, King of Scotland, 11th cent. — Juvenile fiction. I. Title

PS8571.A889 C5 2000   jC813'.54   C00-920165-3
PZ7.K15746 CO 2000

First reprint, 2001

   2 3 4 5 6 7 8 9 10

COTEAU BOOKS
401-2206 Dewdney Ave.
Regina, Saskatchewan
Canada   S4R 1H3

AVAILABLE IN THE US FROM
General Distribution Services
4500 Witmer Industrial Estates
Niagara Falls, NY, 14305-1386

The publisher gratefully acknowledges the financial assistance of the Saskatchewan Arts Board, the Canada Council for the Arts, the Government of Canada through the Book Publishing Industry Development Program (BPIDP), and the City of Regina Arts Commission, for its publishing program.

The Canada Council for the Arts
Le Conseil des Arts du Canada

SASKATCHEWAN ARTS BOARD

Canada

city of Regina

this book is for Doug

Chapter One

He could not see his own body. A while ago there had been a terrible light in his eyes. Maybe it had blinded him.

But no. He could see a patch of moonlit heather and five large stones, tall and dagger-shaped. He turned his head slightly and saw more stones, some standing, some not. A ring of them, he thought. A circle, with him in the middle.

If the stones had all been upright, if they had not looked so old, he might have thought he knew this Goddess Ring.

He wiggled his fingers, and the movement brought a throbbing pain to one palm. Memory flared: something hot in his hand, something perilous.... It was gone now.

He remembered other things: the campfires of Malcolm's men ringing the hills, the loneliness and gloom of the small beechwood where the ragged remnants of his own forces tried to rest, the acrid smouldering of funeral pyres that would not burn clean in the reedy damp of Lumphanan Bottom. But he could not remember how he had burned his hand, or how he had become invisible to his own eyes, or how he had come here.

Nearby he could see a clump of stinging nettles. A couple of strides ought to take him there. Could they sting an invisible man? He made himself smile. It would make a good song: the King of Alba deliberately walking into nettles to see how much of him was alive.

He struck out, one invisible foot in front of the other. It felt strange. "Fool," he muttered to himself, "how many night marches have you made over the years? You saw as little of yourself then."

Night marches. Cattle raids on moonless nights, the boyish rough-and-tumble afterward, hands ruffling his hair in praise. Another night, not so pleasant: fifteen years old and fleeing his father's murderers through darkness. And then, years later, a night march to Sgain, where they would crown him in the dead butcher Duncan's place.

It was fitting that he had begun his rule of Alba on one night march and had seen the beginning of its end on another. Retreating from his hall at Dunsinane the night the traitor Malcolm stormed it, he had known what was to come. It had taken three years, but it was finally at hand. Last night he had stood at the ford of the Dee and watched the drovers' road over the mountains turn bright with the torches of Malcolm's advance. Last night, he had known that he was finished.

Tomorrow all this land would be Malcolm's. For a while, perhaps, Malcolm would pretend he meant Alba to continue as a separate country, but in the end his upbringing in the English court would tell. English nobles would be granted Alban lands and preferences, English laws would take precedence over Alban, rich English bishops would trip their dainty feet down the aisles of Culdee churches. In the end even the name of Alba would vanish. Already some people were calling it Scottiland.

And meanwhile, the King of Alba walked invisible toward a clump of nettles in a ring of stones in a place he did not remember.

One foot in front of the other. How many strides? He had lost count. The nettles were no closer. He walked faster. The heather, the stones, were exactly where they had been; the nettles no nearer at all. There seemed to be no air to breathe. He walked on, though he no longer expected the sudden brush of nettles against his knees. He walked for a long, long time. And he knew all the time that he was going nowhere at all.

He stopped at last. His heart thudded within him. Slowly it calmed. He sat down. He could not feel the ground beneath him.

Outside, in that place of heather and standing stones, clouds netted the moon. Shadows flickered over the turf. The wind was rising. He could hear the rustle of it in the heather and nettles, but felt no breeze himself.

If this was death, neither the old religion nor the Culdees had ever described it so. It was more like a fireside tale of enchantment, of magic spells and sorcery.

Sorcery.

Like a lightning flash, he remembered. Witches. A looking glass. A young girl. A Goddess Ring. The images were flooding in now; he had no control over them. Today's battle, the stream flowing red and Malcolm withdrawing in triumph at nightfall to wait for dawn. Himself, thinking and thinking and no way out and thinking while all around the beauty of the bracken-tang and the loam springy underfoot and the beeches dappled with moonlight made him want to weep. And in his head, creeping like a sickness, the knowledge that there was one way out after all.

Sorcery. A looking glass. A Goddess Ring. Witches.

The three witches had often offered him help during the seventeen years of his reign. He had never accepted. He didn't trust them; their magic was old and dark, nothing to do with enlightened men and their laws and duties. For centuries no Alban monarch had worshipped their Goddess. He himself had been born to the Christ worship, and had no intention of changing. That had not stopped the Goddess's followers from approaching him. However often he turned them away, they kept coming back to him, always at a time of crisis when he might have been tempted.

They had been at his side last night, watching Malcolm's army on the drovers' road. He had heard their whispered offer. It had been the hardest thing he'd ever done to refuse.

He had expected them to come to him tonight. They hadn't. They were nearby, he had been told, in the Goddess Ring in the next valley. He wondered why, tonight of all nights, they were not at his side.

Walking alone in that beechwood, smelling the bitter smoke of his friends' cremations while Malcolm's men laughed in the hills, he had known what he had to do. For one who believed in the Christ God, it was damnation. But Alba was at stake, and he was Alba's king. He would go to the witches and take their Goddess' help, and if he was damned to hell for it, so it must be.

He had gone alone. They were at some private sorcery when he got there. The three witches – one just past her first youth, one middle-aged, the last wrinkled and haggish – had with them a young girl. They also had a mirror. Something about the scene sickened him. Perhaps it was the blue light glittering from the mirror's smooth surface, or perhaps the greed in the young girl's eyes. He had to force himself to enter the Goddess Ring. They turned on him. He was frightened then, but got out his request firmly and respectfully.

The oldest of the witches shrugged. "This night we are about our own affairs. Seek us tomorrow."

He had argued, hopelessly. In the end they'd sent him away. For years they had promised him aid, but now, when he had to have it, when nothing else would save his country, they'd sent him away.

He went, but not far. He could not catch his breath; he had to sit down. He dropped to the ground in a dingle where he could still hear the witches. He was cold. His whole body trembled. He stretched out on his back, staring through treetops to the moon. His palms touched soil. It was thin soil, pebbly hard; you had to work it and work it, for it grew stones more easily than crops. He stroked it. Alba. Oh my Alba.

The English King Edward was supporting Malcolm's bid for the Alban throne; neighbouring kings did such things, you couldn't hate them for it. But Malcolm! Setting English warriors on his own homeland!

Loathing surged through him, red blood and hate pounding against eardrums already pulsing with the noises from the Goddess

Ring. He got to his feet. He didn't know he was going back to the witches until he got to the outer edge of the standing stones. There, still trembling, he stopped. They were deep in their sorcery now, and he could not, he dared not, enter.

He could not go away, either. He hid himself behind a stone and watched. His sickness at what they were doing grew, though for a long time he didn't understand fully what they were about. The haggish witch said something and did something; he could not take his eyes off her. The full moon filled the mirror and spilled azure light over the circle. It was the same glittering blue as the Hag's cold eyes.

All at once the light flared, and the Hag was gone. He knew where; he didn't understand how, but he knew she was inside the mirror.

A blue shimmer returned to the Goddess Ring. He watched the young girl hugging herself as the two remaining witches gave her Words to speak into the glass. He heard those Words. Shuddering, he understood at last this rite that they were performing.

The Hag's body was too old. It had served her for centuries, since before Columba brought the Christ worship from the west. Her aging had been slow but irreversible, and now she needed a new body to inhabit. That was what the young girl was for.

The King of Alba stared at the maiden. She was actually pleased! Didn't she understand? When she repeated that spell they had given her, she too would disappear inside the looking glass. And when she and the Hag came out, it would be the Hag who would wear her own blue-black hair and glowing young skin, and she the body of the Hag.

Perhaps the girl imagined that she would be sharing her body with the Hag, instead of giving it over to her entirely. Or maybe she thought a body was all she was. With the Hag inhabiting that body, it would live for centuries, exerting the Hag's power. Maybe the girl thought that would give *her* power. That must be it. She had been deceived. They were using her, and when they got what they wanted from her they would abandon her.

As the English would abandon Alba. As the witches had already abandoned him.

His temples throbbed. Sweat beaded his forehead. It was not the maiden's fault. She was greedy and ambitious and stupid, but she didn't deserve this fate.

He didn't deserve his own.

His fingernails dug into a crack in the stone in front of him. They tore and bled, but he only dug harder. The witches could have helped him. They had always said they would. But when he needed them, when he'd humbled himself to ask them, when they were his last chance, his only chance....

His fingers dug stone, harder, harder. Through slitted eyes he stared at the two witches, at the girl. When he was dust and Alba English, the three witches would remain. And one of them would be in that child's body — renewed, starting over, while he, while Alba....

Nowhere left to go, only this Goddess Ring, that girl....

Blindly, he was moving. Stop it. Have to stop it. No time to plan. Just do it. This first. And this. The girl shrieking. This is for you, stop it, you'll see it's for the best, stop. One of the witches curled on the ground. Gagging noises. The other clawing, then on her back. The looking glass...quick. Now, yes, hands on the mirror, now! Words, then; witch words in his own voice, but changed to suit himself. Light! Eyes and hand, burning, burning, he couldn't grip the handle any longer, he had to let go....

And then, this place, inside but not inside a Goddess Ring.

Out in the heather the wind was still blowing. He listened to it wearily. A long time passed. The wind died, and still he sat, head on his knees. Outside, in the stone circle, the sun began to rise.

Something stirred near him. He did not see

it or hear it. Rather, he felt it. Alerted by the feeling, he cocked his head on one side. He could see nothing, but he could feel another presence. Someone else was waking, not outside there in that other world of heather and standing stones, but here, inside, with him.

And whoever it was knew he was there, too, and hated him.

For a moment he didn't understand. Then, suddenly, he did.

It was the oldest of the witches, the Hag. She had been inside the looking glass when he'd taken hold of it. She hadn't had time to come out before he had said those Words. And now he was with her.

"Hag," he said, or tried to say. "Are we in the mirror?" No voice, no sound. He was deaf and dumb and blind, but somewhere, he felt the Hag laugh.

So he was right. He was inside the looking glass. He had interfered with Goddess magic, and now he was its prisoner.

You will never get out. You will never be free. Not an actual voice, but the words were sharp in his mind. *This glass will let you see your Alba, but you yourself are gone from it forever.*

He would not listen to her. He would use his brain. He would think of something. Obviously the Hag could use her own magic to get out of the mirror, just as she had used it to get in. But she wasn't attempting to get out. She was staying here in the mirror with him, hating it, and hating him. Why?

He made himself work it out. Outside, the Goddess Ring was empty. It was the same Goddess Ring; he knew it now, though somehow it was changed from the time he had charged into it in the middle of the witches' spell. The two other witches and the young girl were gone. That must be why the Hag was still here. She had only that aged, decrepit body to take to the real world with her. She was afraid to go out, afraid that in the real world her body would die before she found her Sisters again. Inside the mirror she wouldn't age any more than she already had. She could afford to wait for her Sisters to get back to the Goddess Ring and perform the mirror-spell again for her — properly, this time.

When they did, he would be ready. He would watch what she did to get out again, and imitate her....

Except that inside the mirror she was invisible to him. What he couldn't see, he couldn't imitate.

Could *she* see *him*? Could she...do things to him? He had gone into the mirror in that girl's stead. Could the Hag take over his body instead of the girl's?

But if she could have done that, surely she

would have done it already. Probably he'd changed the Words enough to prevent that, though not enough to stop him going into the mirror.

It was disturbing that the other two witches had left the Goddess Ring. Where had they gone? Maybe the young girl had run away after he had taken the mirror from her, and they had gone after her. But then, why hadn't they taken the mirror with them? They hadn't, clearly. If he and the Hag were inside the mirror, and they could see the Goddess Ring, then the mirror must still be in the Goddess Ring.

He blinked into the real world of heather and nettles and saw that it was dawn. On the riverbank, Malcolm would be attacking the last of those loyal to their King. And their King was not with them. He could not get there. His allies would die thinking he had deserted them.

He closed his eyes. When he opened them again there was a boy and a girl in the Goddess Ring. They were leaning against one another, calf-eyed with love. They seemed totally unaware of the world around them. Their garments were odd, the girl's high-collared and long-skirted, the boy in stockings that went all the way up his legs to a puffed tunic ruffling his skinny bottom. No tartans. No breeks. An unfamiliar kind of dagger at his side instead of a sword, useless in battle.

"I will wed thee, Annie." It was the boy, turning a flushed face down to the girl's. His voice was very young.

She stepped back, giving a teasing flounce to her skirts. "I'll wed wi' no actor," she replied, "especially not thee, Thomas Mardell. Thou'rt off to England, where folk are all heathen. I'll not wed thee."

"Thou wilt, though," he said. "I will have no luck playing any stage without thee to watch me."

She laughed. "Take thou white heather for luck instead. Or –" Her hand clutched his arm. "Thomas, look there. There, by that fallen stone. That glint – like light, or an eye...."

His hand went to his dagger, then relaxed. "It's but a looking glass, Annie. Here, I'll get it for thee."

A moment went by, then something happened, a giddy moment like being a child swung in the air. For the first time since waking invisible in that place of nothingness, the King of Alba thought he was being looked at. In return he saw a girl's face, pale braids wound around her head, clear light eyes.

The boy's face came near, too. "See, Annie? Some other lass has been prinking here today."

"She'll not be pleased at losing her glass," the girl said.

"It's a dismal lass that's shed tears for the

loss of this," the boy said disparagingly. "It's old, and the handle's burnt." He made as if to toss it away.

The girl's hand reached out, stopping him. "The glass is good," she said, "good enough for an actor's preening." She twinkled at him. "Take it to England, and thou'lt have all thou needst o' Scotland."

"I will take it," he said, "an' I'll take thee, too — one for preening, and t'other for sense."

Laughter. More kisses. A flurry of movement, a dizzying blur.

Then darkness. Darkness for a long, long time.

⌘ ⌘ ⌘

SHE HAD BEEN AFRAID, and she had been bored. Above all, she had been lonely. There was a man in the mirror with her, but after that first moment of her strange awakening in the Goddess Ring she had refused to acknowledge him. He was a male who had interfered with a Goddess Power, and if what she suspected was true, the results did not stop with mere sacrilege.

Where were her two Sisters? The full moon had come and gone a dozen times since that boy and girl had taken the looking glass away from the Goddess Ring, but still her Sisters had not come. It was not because the glass had been moved, for its attracting force was sufficient to draw anyone who served the Goddess, given enough time. Was a year not enough? Or had something happened to obstruct her Sisters?

Most of the time the two young lovers who had taken the glass kept it covered up. The few times she had been able to look out had filled her with unease. She knew nothing of the place they had called England, but if this was that place, it was a greatly different from everything she understood. That and the long, dark periods flayed her nerves almost as much as the desperate attempts at companionship from the man with her in the mirror. She could not, she would not, stay in the dark with him, away from the breath of earth and moon, forever.

A year was long enough. She would go out.

It was a terrible risk. She had been too old before. Inside the mirror a dozen months had aged her not at all, but once she left the mirror she would age all twelve months at once. And if the thing she feared was true, she could die of old age the moment the spell took effect.

That fear had kept her here all this time, but now she had to know. She summoned her Power.

Now.

A wide platform, higher than the audience below. Two men, painted faces, strange garb, harshly projected voices. One had just pulled the looking glass out from under his cloak. He dropped it with a clatter when she materialized out of it, and fell to his knees, white with horror.

The mob hooted and clapped appreciatively. "Flummoxed him proper, that did. Ho, Granny, next time warn him about that trapdoor!"

"Strewth but there's an ancient! Eyes rheumy as a mill-wheel. Those wrinkles are not all from the powder-pot, or I'm a player myself."

Old. Oh, old. Bent double. *Blind, too? Or just tears?*

"Forgotten your lines, Granny?" someone shouted.

"So have they all, seems like."

Her arms hung almost to the wooden floor of the stage. Feebly she made a sweep with one of them, feeling for the mirror. Spittle streaked her chin. Her breath came in ragged gasps. *Too old. Must go back. Must go....*

Her swollen knuckles brushed the handle of the mirror. Slowly and painfully she closed it into her palm. It gave her strength. She began to straighten.

"Put that looking glass down!" a fat man yelled authoritatively. "And stop bothering my actors! I'll have no females on my stage, old woman."

"What's he talking about? That's just one of the actors, isn't it?"

And then, somehow, they knew. "That's no actor. She wasn't there, and then she was. She's a witch! Kill her!"

It would have to be a masking spell. She could manage that. Even a Maiden could — even so tired, even with no moon — but a Maiden could run, and that mob was already surging up the steps.... *Don't look at them. Think the words. Think.* She made the moon in her mind. She made silence. *Yes. Yes.* A walk, wheezing and trembling. *They cannot see you.* The balcony at the rear of the stage. Behind it, actors. Two, three. *They do not see you.* A wooden staircase. One step down; pause, gasping for breath; another step; another. The mob behind, howling for blood. A doorway to the street. *Walk. Walk. They cannot see you. Walk.*

The nearest cottage, an opening spell, a quiet room, a desk. She sank into a chair, closing her eyes. Pain in her chest, fierce as a brand. *Breathe. Breathe.* She gripped the mirror and breathed. Time passed. She half-opened her eyes, letting her gaze rest on the desk.

A quill pen. She touched it leadenly. There was a pile of loose pieces of paper under it. Beside this pile was a sheaf of pages bound together between leather covers. Words were printed on the leather. CRONIKLES OF ENGLAND, SCOTLAND AND IRELAND. HOLINSHED. She read the words mechanically, a Goddess skill she had known since she was Maiden. They meant nothing to her. She read the words on the top sheet of the pile under the pen, too. These meant as little, and were badly scrawled and blotted, but somehow she could not so easily pass them by. TH* TRA**DIE *F MACB***. By W'L**M****SPEAR*.

And under that: A**O DO**** 1606.

She read the last part twice, breathing harshly, out, in. This at least she understood. Anno Domini, 1606. It was how they named the years, these people not of the Goddess. When she had last been in the Goddess Ring with her Sisters the year was Anno Domini, 1057.

Five hundred and fifty years between that time and this. Her deepest fear had been right.

She had guessed it, but still the rage flooded her. She knew what had happened. She knew the man responsible. They had refused him help in his petty little war, and he had taken his revenge. He had wrenched the glass away from the girl when the spell was already primed, and then he had changed the final words. Only two small changes, wisely chosen or the spell would have failed altogether, but enough. His first alteration had been to the ordering of the words "past" and "future". "Find through this glass a future for thy past," he had said, rather than "a past for thy future," as had been meant, and here she was, not in a younger body but an older one, her own grim future. And his second alteration....

With swollen, gnarled fingers she brushed aside the top sheet on the pile of papers. Under it was more of that spiky, inky scrawl. But now she was concentrating, and the Goddess was with her. She knew what she was reading. A drama. Someone here was writing one of those entertainments for the masses, like the one she had materialized into, or the passion plays the Christ Church favoured. And she knew what this drama was about. It was about the man who shared her own mirror prison.

There was great power in the mirror. It had heard the King of Alba's words, and brought him to this unquiet future where his name lived on. That had been his second change to the Words of Power — that his own name, rather than the Goddess's, would not be forgotten.

There were only four pages so far. She read them again, her gnarled fingers curling with fury at the kindness with which the man had been remembered. But at the end of the first scene the unknown writer had added a note to himself in a darker ink, taking time over it, underscoring it twice. *Not cert'n about this. This M. has no flaws. Chk Holinshed.*

She smiled grimly to herself, reading that. The playwright had written a hero, but his

instinct told him it was villains who were interesting. Well, she could help him with that.

She opened the book with the name
Holinshed on it. A few scraps of cloth inside
marked particular pages. She turned to them,
read, nodded. It was a history; the unknown
playwright was using it as his source for this
play. For her purposes it needed a change or
two. She closed her eyes and focused on the
Goddess within her. When she opened her eyes
again it was so nearly dark she had to squint to
read the pages in front of her. She smiled, lin-
gering over each word. The changes were good,
stylish, undetectable. She flicked the leather
cover closed with a soft and final thud.

You wanted your name to be remembered, she told
the man in the mirror. *Now I've made sure that it
will be.*

She took the mirror from her lap, where it
had rested face down against her rags. As she
lifted it, moonlight slanted in through a nearby
window, catching the glass in a wink of blue.
She smiled savagely at her own hideous reflection. She'd been ugly enough before, but that
was nothing to what she was now, after aging
five hundred and fifty years in the space of time
it took to come out of the mirror. Ugly outside, uglier inside. Lungs blackened with
growths, heart labouring to push blood
through veins narrowed to hairs, half-paralysed

on one side, joints deformed. She would be dead in another day if she stayed outside the mirror. The Goddess-power gave immensely long life to the mortal bodies of Sisters, but it couldn't make them live forever. She would have to go back inside the mirror where she could wait in unaging nothingness until her two Sisters found the mirror and provided her a new body to wear.

They would search for the mirror, of course. And not just because of her. A great part of their joint power had gone into the mirror to prime the transfer spell. It would remain there until the spell was completed. As well, her Sisters needed to get the mirror back for their own eventual transfers to younger bodies.

But her Sisters lived now five and a half centuries in the past. They would have to survive five hundred and fifty years before they could begin their real search for the mirror, because its physical existence had leaped all those centuries. After that the mirror would draw them to it, but it might be a slow attraction, and every day their bodies would grow older. Goddess let them live long enough to find her!

Maybe she could help. A hint. Something to draw her Sisters more quickly to the mirror's location.

She looked again at the scrawled first scene

of the unknown writer's drama. He would change it when he came back to it because of what she had done to his "Holinshed." She could influence him further, make him decide to use this mirror in his drama, suggest a phrase or two that would draw her Sisters' attention. When he came, she would try it. But not in this body. This body could wait no longer.

She moved the mirror on the desk so that the moonlight struck it full in the glass. She drew the last shreds of her strength to her. It was time.

Power flared blue. The room was empty.

The mirror sat on the desk, dull now, the moonlight gone from it.

It was dawn before anyone came. He was a long-faced man, intelligent, tired-looking. He came straight to the desk when he entered the room. He rubbed his balding head, tugged at the solitary earring he wore, and frowned, see-ing the mirror.

"Someone's been here," he muttered.

He sat down, fiddled with the handle of the mirror, then picked up the first two sheets of manuscript. Reading, he frowned, then said aloud, "I do not care what Holinshed says, the truth does not read like truth. I cannot...."

He paused, then dropped the page. He turned his head, staring for rather a long time at the mirror. Then he opened up the leather-bound Holinshed, turning to the marked pages. He read, gave an exclamation, and read some more. Then, almost feverishly, he pushed aside the Holinshed, picked up his quill and a fresh sheet of paper, and wrote.

When shall we three meet again? In thunder, lightning, or in rain?

"Whatever happens after this," he murmured happily as he scribbled, "my troth, but it begins well!"

Canada

Chapter Two

"KINCARDINE?" BEHIND THE GLASS WALL of his booth the doorman chewed the name over, looking down on Kinny thoughtfully. "Kincardine. Funny name for a girl. There's a town called that. On Lake Huron."

"There's one in Scotland that's got my last name *and* my first," Kinny said. "O'Neil," she added, to remind him, "Kincardine O'Neil."

"Two names for a town?" the man said. "Sounds funny to me."

Kinny shifted impatiently. "They said at the box office to come here. They said you'd have my name on a list."

The phone rang. While the doorman answered it, Kinny stood on tiptoe to try to see if there was a paper with her name on it anywhere in the booth. She was tall, but the booth was six steps up from the orange-tiled lobby floor, and she couldn't see much. Kinny wondered if they had designed it like that to make visitors feel small. You had to expect things to be larger than life at the Stratford Festival Theatre, even at the stage door.

The guard had put down the phone and was

looking at Kinny again. "You did say someone was expecting you?"

His tone was perfectly courteous, but she was sure he thought she was just a stagestruck kid looking for autographs. "I'm working for Jeneva Strachan this summer," she said very clearly. "I'm her assistant for this season's *Macbeth*. She knew I was coming today. If you page her, you'll —"

"I can't page her. She's in rehearsal. And if you're an assistant director, I'm Laurence Olivier. You look about fourteen."

"I'm sixteen," Kinny said, "and even if I weren't, some of the most important things in the world are being done by young people these days." She gave him a straight look, very green, from under her dark eyebrows.

His eyes began to twinkle. "You can speak up for yourself, anyway, Miss Kincardine-like-the-town O'Neil. But you don't know beans about the theatre if you can call the Scottish play by its real name *here!*"

Kinny flushed. She was going to be an actor. She had wangled her way into the theatre arts course of her Montreal high school five semesters in a row now, and had starred in the school show three years running. She had read every theatre biography she could get her hands on. Next March, whatever her parents said, she'd be taking the auditions for the National

Theatre School, and even if they did accept only sixteen students a year from all across Canada, she was sure she would get in. How could she have forgotten that it was bad luck to call *Macbeth* by its real name on theatre premises?

If you wanted to talk about *Macbeth*, you had to call it "the Scottish play." And if you talked about the man Macbeth, you had to give him a nickname: the Thane, or Mac, or sometimes, jokingly, the Big Mackers. It was because so many bad things had happened over the years to people involved with productions of the play. All over the world, wherever the play was put on, there were accidents to actors and backstage crew, or there were serious illnesses, directors got fired, or producers went bankrupt. Even unfavourable reviews were put down to the famous *Macbeth* bad luck. Nor was the audience immune to the *Macbeth* curse. Kinny's drama teacher had told them about an opening night where the man right in front of him had a heart attack at the exact moment of King Duncan's death.

Some people said *Macbeth* was bad luck because Shakespeare had given his three witches in the play a real witches' curse to say. Whatever the reason, Kinny thought now, it looked as if she was getting her share of the luck today. She'd forgotten and called the play by its real name, and now after coming all the way from Montreal the guard wasn't even going to let her in.

"I've been on a train all day," she told him. "I've read...the Scottish play...six times this past week alone. Jeneva Strachan has hired me to help her with it this summer. I've got the letter here from her, if you want to look." She scrabbled in her bag, found the letter, and held it out.

He waved it away. "I guess I believe you," he said, smiling.

Kinny blinked in surprise. "Then can I —?"

"No interrupting rehearsals." He looked at her curiously. "How'd you manage to get a job that theatre people twice your age would kill for?"

"Genius?" Kinny suggested. She tried for a modest shrug.

The guard laughed. "Pull, huh? I thought so."

It was what everyone here would think, Kinny knew. The worst of it was that it was true. Her mother had been Jeneva Strachan's best friend in high school. They still exchanged cards at Christmas, and for years Jeneva brought her various men friends over for dinner. Kinny always sat silent and big-eyed at those meals, watching the way Jeneva flourished her fork with one hand while the long index finger of the other flicked crumbs away, physical punctuation marks for the beautifully orated opinions projected effortlessly to the far corners of the house. With her odd, crooked smile, one eyebrow higher than the other, and her painfully short sand-coloured hair, she wasn't at all beautiful. But Kinny couldn't stop looking at her. Mom could say all she wanted about Jeneva's makeup, her one earring instead of two, her loose-fitting, expensive clothes, her turnstile of men. Jeneva was an actor. You couldn't expect actors to be ordinary.

And then Jeneva had stopped acting and become a stage director, and in her congratulations card Mom had written something about stage directing and playing God, and communications back and forth had stopped. They would probably never have started up again if it hadn't been for Kinny telling her parents about the National Theatre School.

"Yes, I know you love the idea of acting," Mom had almost wailed. "But that's just fun, not real life. What happened to ecology? Greenpeace isn't my idea of a great career but it's better than —"

"There's no money in acting." That was Dad, of course.

"— though I never thought you'd stick with nursing, you're too squeamish, but if you'd specialized in the elderly the way you said...Kinny, you were going to save the world! Animal rights, remember? Acting's not going to —"

"If it meant she would stop marching in the streets with French signs — and why in hell she thinks the French need any help at all, let alone from an English kid —"

"— and remember the time you tried to get your student council to adopt a street person? That awful girl you kept inviting for dinner even though she pretended not to understand a word of English? One cause after another, as if you're the only person in the world who can see anything wrong or try to fix it. People don't *like* people like that. Who wants to be friends with Joan of Arc? When you got involved in your first school show I was so relieved — an activity that was just plain fun, for a change. I should have known you'd turn it into another burning passion. Anyway, there's no work for Anglophone actors in Quebec, you'd have to move away."

Later that same night Kinny had overheard her father and mother talking. "What Kinny needs is a dose of reality," Dad had said. "A summer job in professional theatre would show her what's what. Hard work for low pay; sweaty costumes and being upstaged by fat old queens with earrings trying to bounce around like juveniles. She'd drop all this nonsense about theatre school once she saw what it's really like.

Why don't you call Jeneva? She's always had a soft spot for Kinny."

Listening, Kinny knew what she should do. She should tell her parents they were wrong about her only being romantic about acting. She should tell them she would make her own way in the theatre. She should tell them she would work at McDonald's this summer and still go to the National Theatre School next spring. But instead, when Jeneva's letter had come, Kinny had accepted a job in the most famous classical theatre in the country, and she had been as excited about it as if she had got the job on her own merits. She was determined that by the end of the summer, she would deserve it.

Again the doorman answered the phone, then turned back to Kinny. "Name's Bill Flynn," he said. "Call me Bill. Want a coffee while you wait for Jeneva? A coke, maybe?"

She shook her head. Her stomach was churning with nervousness and excitement. She sat down on one of the blue chairs that lined the wall below Bill Flynn's booth. The stage door opened and a burly man entered, carrying a crate. "For Jim Simpson." he said. "Props."

"Right," Bill said. "I'll see he gets it."

The burly man went away. Kinny looked at the loudspeaker, the bulletin board, the pay phone, the ashtray full of butts. She walked over and read a plaque on the wall, but couldn't remember what it said the moment she'd finished. Just ahead was a long corridor ending at double glass doors. A sign on one of the doors said: NOTICE. NO ENTRY UNLESS AUTHORIZED. Some large stage props were behind the door. There was an enormous tube, big as a child's slide. Beside it a huge Roman-looking plaster head stared calmly out from under a crown of laurel. Kinny looked longingly at the double doors, then turned her head to the doorman's glass booth. Bill Flynn was watching her. He grinned. She wrinkled her nose at him, went back to the blue chair, and waited some more. After a little while she shifted her chair so that she could see down the corridor to the double doors.

One of the doors opened, and three men came into view. They were talking loudly over a violin playing somewhere in the theatre behind them. "I don't get it. Last season's production brought in so many big bucks. Why change it?" The speaker was a man with smooth, boyish cheeks and the kind of voice Kinny thought of as deliberately sexy.

"A French-versus-English version will shake up the critics," another man said cynically. "It'll get a lot of press."

"But the money!" The first speaker again. "Brand-new costumes for everyone, a whole new design, and all of it costing. Revivals are supposed to be cheap. That's what they do them for. I wonder how she got the Board to agree?"

"Get with it, Norris," the cynical one said. He had a youthful mop of angelic dark curls, a strange contrast to his knowing, sardonic features. "You've been around. Hell, you're understudying the lead! You must know you can persuade a theatre board to fund just about anything if you mention the Edinburgh Festival, followed by Paris and Munich."

Kinny's ears pricked up. *Macbeth* was going to the Edinburgh Festival in August. She would be going with it, Jeneva had said. Were these men talking about *Macbeth*?

The three men had reached the stage door now. The one who hadn't said anything yet leaned negligently against the door jamb, seeming in a world of his own as the other two lit up cigarettes. The cynical one inhaled smoke greedily. "God, I thought she'd never let us take a break. Have you ever spent so much time going over a design?"

"Interesting, though," the smooth-faced Norris said. "I liked the big M's costumes."

The big M. Kinny nodded to herself. So it was her play they were talking about.

"You won't get a chance to wear them, Norris." Smoke wreathed the second young man's tousled head. He grinned like a satyr, and Kinny decided she didn't like him. "Alexander Blair never gets sick." He turned to the third man, the silent one. "What do you say, Lucas? Want to put money on it that Norris never sets foot on the stage as our Thane?"

The one called Lucas shrugged. "No bet." Kinny thought she had never seen anyone so self-contained. He was rather short for an actor, really not much taller than she was. His body seemed to be composed mostly of angles, his face too sharp-boned to be handsome. He couldn't be more than twenty.

"You're so jealous, Adam," Norris said complacently.

"Not of you," was the swift reply. "And not of Alex Blair, either. If Jeneva's hot little idea for this production doesn't work it'll be Alex who'll get buried in the manure."

"Jeneva's done a lot of research," Norris pointed out.

"Which will definitely not cut it in Quebec. They're not going to like the evil big Mac dressed as Montcalm. One of their most beloved heroes, if I may remind you. And war-torn Scotland transplanted to Quebec's own Plains of Abraham —" Adam shook his head "— it's political dynamite."

Lucas spoke up then. "You Canadians may know a lot about the Battle of the Plains of

Abraham," he said, in a harsh, deep voice that seemed as if it should go with a much older man, "but it isn't only going to be Canadians we're performing it for. What will the Europeans know about Canadian history?" He was still leaning against the door, one knee bent so that his foot rested on it. "And anyway, what does Canada have to do with a play Shakespeare wrote before he knew Canada existed?"

"You Americans still don't think Canada exists," said Adam. "We're just the place the cold weather comes from."

Lucas looked amused. "On dull days we while away the hours thinking about the RCMP musical ride, too," he offered.

"But the grape-vine says your parents were French-Canadian, Lucas," Adam said to him. "Why don't you know some Canadian history? About the Plains of Abraham, for instance?"

Yes, Kinny thought, why doesn't he?

"It doesn't matter what *I* know," Lucas said coolly. "What matters is if anybody besides us can figure out why Jeneva's staging the Scottish play in eighteenth-century Canada."

"Lucas has got a point," Norris put in. "I'm Canadian, and I don't know if *I* understand what she's up to. I studied the Battle of the Plains of Abraham in school, but all I remember is that Wolfe defeated Montcalm and took

Quebec City for the English. In the Scottish play Malcolm defeats the Big Mac, so I suppose it makes a bit of sense that Malcolm's going to be dressed as Wolfe, and the Big Mac as Montcalm —"

"There've been a lot more battles in history than the Plains of Abraham," Lucas interrupted. "The Big M could have been dressed as Hitler and Wolfe as Churchill, if Jeneva wanted to make some kind of modern parallel. Why this one?"

Adam stubbed out his cigarette. "It's personal to Jeneva," he said. "She hates Quebec."

No way, Kinny thought. Jeneva had grown up in Quebec. How could she hate it?

"What does that have to do with —?"

"Think about it, Lucas. In the play you've got an evil Scottish king who kills just about everybody, then is killed himself. Order is restored *by the English,* and everything is happy. The end. Translate evil Scottish king to evil French-Canadian leader, and you've got the picture. Jeneva sees French Quebec as a canker on our fair land. Only the English can make our country right. The maple leaf forever, and God Save the Queen."

No, Kinny thought. Her hands twisted in her lap. It couldn't be.

"I didn't know Jeneva was anti-French," Norris said slowly.

"Jeneva's an anglophone who lived in Quebec," Adam said. "What do you expect, the way the English are being treated there? Like second-class citizens...."

"So Jeneva's making a political statement with this play?" Lucas demanded. "She's using our play to tell the French what she thinks of them?"

"Don't sound so outraged," Adam said, amused. "Most of Canada will agree with her. They've had just about enough of Quebec's banning English signs and forcing immigrants to go to French schools even when they want to learn English. And everybody in Canada's fed up with having to read French on their breakfast cereal boxes. We've given and given to those frogs over the years and all they do is croak for more."

That was it. Kinny scrambled to her feet. She was so angry, she was shaking. "Frogs!" she burst in. "You bigoted – you –" All three of the men were staring at her in astonishment. She didn't care. "Maybe *you'd* be fed up with reading *English* on your cereal boxes if you were French," she got out, very fast. "Maybe if you'd grown up French in a province where the English ran everything even though they make up only 10 percent of the population, where you had to speak English to get a job serving your own people –"

She broke off. Even Bill Flynn in his glass booth was gaping at her.

"You speak English awfully well for a Francophone," Adam said.

"I'm not Francophone," Kinny said. "You don't have to be a Francophone to know what's right and what isn't. We English have treated the French Canadians like dirt. A dose of our own medicine isn't so unfair."

"Ever hear of reverse discrimination, sweetie?"

"Leave it, Adam," said Lucas. "She's only a kid."

A kid! Kinny turned on him. "What about you? You're French-Canadian. What do you think about all this?"

"I'm not French-Canadian. I'm American."

"Your parents were French-Canadian. I heard the others say so."

"I was born in Cohoes, New York. My parents always spoke English to me. They left Canada years before I was born. I don't know anything about your local politics, and frankly, I don't much care."

"Don't care! What's wrong with you? It's not local politics, it's your heritage. It's what you are!"

"What I am," Lucas said coolly, "is an actor." He turned to the other men. "Break's over in a minute. God Incarnate'll be on our tails if we're late getting back."

"Sorry, lambkin," Adam told Kinny cheerfully, "you'll have to vent your pro-French emotions on someone else. Just count yourself lucky you don't have to deal with a certain director I know. She'd *really* have you in a rage, the views she has."

But dealing with Jeneva Strachan was just exactly what she was going to have to do, Kinny thought glumly. She watched the men going back through the glass door. Funny how Lucas's angular body lost all its sharp edges when he moved. How dare he toss away his French-Canadian ancestry like an old sock full of holes?

She was startled by Bill Flynn's voice. "You really gave it to them, didn't you?"

She turned to him suspiciously, but he only grinned. "Actors can be a pain," he said. "So damn full of themselves, they can't see anything but mirrors." He winked. "I'll just have a try for Jeneva now, before rehearsal starts again." He began dialling.

Jeneva. Again Kinny's heart sank. She was here in Stratford as Jeneva's assistant. That meant she was going to have to connive at an anti-French *Macbeth*. The main character dressed up like the Quebec General Montcalm. And Montcalm had been a good man, not a murderer like *Macbeth*! Kinny hated the idea. But she wasn't going to keep her job unless she managed to keep her mouth shut. Already there were three men in the cast who knew she wouldn't like this production. Would they tell Jeneva?

Whether they did or not, she was going to have to work with them. "A great way to start your summer job, Kincardine," she muttered to herself.

"You're to go down to Rehearsal Hall 3," said the doorman, hanging up the telephone. "The easiest way is go outside." He gave her directions, then added conspiratorially, "A word to the wise, huh? Maybe you've done enough speaking up for yourself for one day?"

Kinny nodded gloomily. "I was just thinking that myself."

Chapter Three

"**T**HAT WAS ONE MOUTHY KID," ADAM SAID to Lucas as they descended the stairs. Norris had gone to get something he had forgotten.

Lucas made himself shrug, but the girl's accusation had stung. What did she know about his heritage? Maybe if she'd been born next to a textiles mill and grown up with a bunch of Franco-American kids who thought Shakespeare was what Indians did on the Amazon, she'd have some right to talk about it. What did she know about schools where they spray-painted "Frenchie Go Home" on your locker even though you'd been born in the U.S. and refused to say a word of French since you were six?

"She didn't know what she was talking about," he answered calmly.

"Does anything get to you, Lucas?" Adam asked curiously. "Other than forgetting your lines, I mean. If you ever did."

"I've only *got* two lines in this play," Lucas said.

"Fleance is a pretty lousy part," Adam agreed smugly. He had eight lines as Donalbain, son of the murdered King Duncan.

He gave Lucas a look, mildly superior. "You haven't had much luck with the roles this summer, have you? I mean Balthasar in *Romeo and Juliet* isn't bad — what, twenty lines —?"

"More like twenty-five."

"— but what do they give you in *Hamlet?* Just an understudy...okay, it's Laertes, but it *is* just an understudy. And Fleance in this. I'd have thought they'd have treated their fair-haired American scholarship boy with more respect."

"I got exactly the roles I expected," Lucas replied, as evenly as he could manage. He had given up wondering why some of the actors here at Stratford seemed to resent his fellowship from the Chicago branch of the Stratford Festival Foundation. The fellowship didn't get him anything but his salary as a member of the Young Company. And it wasn't as if the fellowship had been handed to him on a platter. He'd sweated bullets getting through the preliminary auditions, and he still had nightmares about the final one, where the Stratford artistic director had picked him from all the finalists. Now that he was here, it was perfectly obvious he wasn't being given any preferential treatment. As Adam said, a couple of bit parts and an understudy weren't exactly a season to rave about. "Lines aren't everything," he added.

Adam smiled wickedly. "So say we all, when we don't get them."

They were in the bottom-floor corridor of the theatre now, threading their way through racks of costumes that had spilled out into the hall from the costume and soft-props work-rooms to the left. Sewing machines were running at high speed. Someone was singing an aria from *Don Giovanni.* A woman with her mouth full of pins came out of the workroom door just as Adam and Lucas walked by. "Sharp-tongued as usual, I see, Doris," Adam said. She glared at him, grabbed an enormous spool of thread from a box waiting to be unloaded, and stalked back into the workroom.

An actor Lucas recognized from *Hamlet* was hurrying down the corridor in front of them, heading for the rehearsal hall. Because so many of the actors at Stratford had parts in more than one play, scheduling rehearsals was tricky. The rehearsals themselves had felt chaotic to Lucas when he first arrived. In Chicago the the-atre he had worked in for the last year had rehearsed and performed a single play at a time, and when a scene was called, everyone who had a part to play in it was there from start to fin-ish. Here actors drifted in as they became avail-able from other shows and hurried out when they were needed more urgently elsewhere, but Lucas had such small roles he'd had almost no scheduling conflicts. Now that both his other shows had the kinks worked out of them, he was free, except for performances, to spend as much time as he wanted at the *Macbeth* rehearsals.

Macbeth was Lucas's favourite play, and the part of Macbeth was one that he'd set his sights on ever since he'd first seen it performed. It wasn't just because it was one of the best parts ever written for an actor. Lucas was fascinated by Macbeth's contradictions. He was a villain whose ambition and treachery led him to murder his king and his best friend, who consorted with witches and summoned up demons and connived at the slaughter of innocent women and children. But still there were things Lucas admired about Macbeth. Dullards can commit murder and not worry about it; but Macbeth knew what he was doing and knew what it would do to him, and he did it anyway. That took courage, Lucas thought, and he admired courage, especially when it came from a man as totally alone as Macbeth. He admired his imagination too. And though he didn't admire Macbeth's actions, he could understand what caused them. He could understand wanting something very much, knowing you could do it better than anyone, and not being able to get what you wanted in the ordinary way. What Lucas couldn't understand was the humanity that remained with Macbeth to the end despite his chosen isolation from human beings. What was it about Macbeth that made the ghost of his best friend torment him, made him want heirs to carry on after him in a world he had virtually destroyed, made him try not to kill Macduff after committing so many other murders? Lucas didn't know. He wouldn't know until he'd had a chance to become Macbeth on stage.

Adam was waylaid by a young actor just outside the door of Rehearsal Hall 3, and Lucas went in without him. This morning a rectangle of chairs had been set up around the perimeter of the room, finishing at a long wooden table piled with scripts and other papers. There was only one chair at this table, and Jeneva Strachan had been sitting in it, solitary as a monarch. She hadn't moved from it for the whole first read-through, making few comments. Everyone but Alexander Blair and Meredith Archer, who were playing Macbeth and his Lady, had sounded dull. But nobody was at all dull at the end, when Jeneva had dropped her bombshell about the French-Canadian interpretation she was going to put on this year's production.

Jeneva was still at the table now, deep in conversation with the set designer. The cast had spent an hour after the lunch break going through costume sketches. Lucas still couldn't get used to the idea of the Scottish Thane wearing the uniform of a French army general instead of tartans. He wanted to take a second look at the drawing at Jeneva's elbow, but hesitated to interrupt her. While he hovered, the stage manager Everett Lunn, known to the company as "God Incarnate", billowed in from the corridor, tapped Jeneva smartly on the shoulder with a portable phone, closed her hand around the receiver, and rolled his elephantine bulk out, all without saying a word. Jeneva shrugged an apology to the designer and spoke into the phone.

"Jeneva Strachan here." Pause. "Oh, yes, Bill, you're our Security for today, aren't you?" Pause. "Hellfire, darling, it wasn't today, surely? The kid's still in school, I thought." Pause. "Well, I suppose there's nothing to be done about it. You'd better send her down." She clicked off the receiving switch, remarking, "Not nearly as satisfying as slamming the bloody thing down when you're in a temper."

"Bad news, Jeneva?" someone asked.

"Totally insignificant, darling. Nuisance value only. God knows why I say yes to these things. Other people outgrow their obligations to high school friendships, but not me." She ran her hand through her brushcut hair and raised her brows questioningly at Lucas. He

48

drifted away.

In ones and twos the cast re-entered the hall. During the break most of the chairs had been stacked away in a corner, and the hall seemed much emptier. The red and blue tape on the floor was easier to see now. It outlined an area the exact size and shape of the real stage upstairs; even the positions of steps and the understage tunnels were marked. The tape made it possible for the cast to rehearse positions "on stage" when the actual stage was in use for other purposes. Lucas had never rehearsed in this hall before, but he'd taken classes in voice and body movement here, and he liked the springy feel of the floor and the ancient and ineradicable aroma of actors' sweat. Peter Ustinov's sweat, he thought, and Maggie Smith's; William Hutt's, Kate Reid's, Brian Bedford's. Now and then he let himself think of his own sweat, mingling with all the others.

Everett Lunn sailed into the hall again, calling "Stand by for Witches' Scene One". He looked at his watch, scribbled something in his red pocket notebook, frowned at an actor changing his shoes by the door, and rumbled, "Quiet, please! Witches, stand by for Scene One: Thunder and Lightning."

An old woman came into the rehearsal hall. She walked jerkily, almost blurrily, like a cartoon movie made with too few drawings to make the viewer see smooth movement. She looked at least a hundred, her face deeply seamed, gullies around her eyes and mouth. Her lips were wide and loose as if they had been stretched by too many teeth. She didn't have too many teeth now but she had beautiful hair, pure white and thick as a scarf, which she wore twisted into an uneven braid that hung down the middle of her back. It was an unkind style, doing nothing to hide the pronounced widow's hump that pushed her head out at a sharp angle to her body. She wore several layers of shapeless wool with all the colour washed out of it, and her body was thick and pear-shaped. She looked, Lucas thought, like someone who had given birth to too many children.

Her expression was wearily impatient, driven and bored at the same time. His mother had often looked like that, Lucas remembered. He thought of the time his sister Michelle had set fire to the oven when she forgot about the cookies she'd begged to be allowed to make; and the day he had left home after lying about his age to get into theatre school in Chicago. "*Oui* you want permission, you want freedom, you want, you want. Me, I just want out." This woman, too, wanted out.

He watched her, puzzled. No one that age could possibly be an actor, or working in any way for the Festival. Yet here she was, in a rehearsal that was closed to the public, and no one said anything to stop her. She didn't seem to expect interference. She had the air of someone who didn't expect other people even to notice her.

Until she saw that he was watching her.

She changed then. Her eyes, a shiny blue-grey that was almost silver, went startlingly pale. She stared at him as if she had never seen a man before. Astonishment and outrage and a kind of desperation chased themselves across her features. Her skin was paper white.

Lucas half got to his feet. "Is there anything –?" he began.

But she hurried on, setting a jerky course for the empty coat rack at one side of the hall. People saw her – they must have seen her – but still no one questioned her presence. Lucas frowned after her, watching her intently. Then something distracted him – a flicker of one of the overhead factory-type lights, or maybe a reflection from the window of the smaller rehearsal hall upstairs – and when he looked for the woman again, she was gone.

"Witches! Stand by!" God Incarnate again, hurrying things up with his usual bellow.

"We're right beside you, Everett," the First Witch said, in a tart Newfoundland accent. "You needn't blow our ears off."

In real life she was Joan Mackenzie, a plump

woman with a kind face, a far cry from the hor-
rific creature Shakespeare had invented to lure
Macbeth to his doom. The Second Witch,
Gwen Park, was middle-aged and just as ordi-
nary-looking. Lucas didn't know either
woman's work except by reputation, which was
good.

The Third Witch was much younger, played
by Christine Gale. Lucas knew her from the
Young Company. She was beautiful in a fine-
boned, spiritual-looking way. She had fluffy
blond hair and round, blue eyes; very different
from his last girlfriend May, with her dark eyes
and deep, earthy laugh. On arriving at Stratford
he had toyed with the idea of asking Christine
out, until he heard her regale half a dozen other
actors in the Green Room with the full tale of
her previous night's date, including the bedroom scene. Lucas had nothing against bedroom scenes, but if he was going to star in one
for an audience, on the whole he preferred that
it be on the stage.

The three witches took their places in the
centre of the rehearsal hall. "Not there," Jeneva
said, leaving her table. She put one index finger
on Christine's shoulder and pointed with the
other. "I want you harder to see. Back."

The three witches moved back. Jeneva nodded. "Good." She returned to her table. "Go."

"'When shall we three meet again?'" Joan

said, giving the First Witch's opening speech. She used her ordinary speaking voice.

"Think French when you say that, darling," Jeneva said.

"You don't want a French accent, do you?" Joan demanded, horrified.

"I don't think we'll go that far. But I don't want you to sound like you've just had a meal of cod and salt pork, either."

🮜 🮜 🮜

THEY HAD FINISHED WITH THE WITCHES, and got to the point where the soldiers tell King Duncan how Macbeth has won the day for them, when the ouside fire door opened. A girl came in. Lucas saw her at once, because he had been watching that corner of the room. A moment before, he had thought he'd seen a dark, humped shadow moving there, a shadow that reminded him vividly of the white-haired, hunchbacked he'd seen earlier. But she couldn't have been there, because the daylight flooding in through the open fire door revealed no one. Lucas frowned, puzzled, then shrugged. He looked again at the girl who had just come in. Lustrous honey-coloured hair strangled in a ponytail, scared green eyes, generous mouth, no makeup, a Save The Whales button pinned defiantly over what was probably a designer logo on the sweatshirt she wore almost to her slender knees. It was that kid from the stage door lounge all right, the one with so many opinions. What was she doing here?

She hesitated in the doorway, clearly taken aback by finding herself in the backstage area of the rehearsal hall, with a rehearsal in progress in front of her. She let the fire door close behind her and, slowly and carefully, began to tiptoe in. There wasn't much room between the door and the backdrop for the rehearsal stage, and she was carrying a big suitcase. In trying to maneuvre around the corner of the backdrop, her suitcase banged into a wall, fell out of her grip, and thudded loudly to the floor.

King Duncan stopped orating.

"More quiet backstage," the stage manager said automatically, and then, taking in the girl's youth and scarlet face, "We're not open to the public, young lady. You've come in a wrong door, I'm afraid."

"I was supposed to...I didn't mean to interrupt rehearsal, but Jeneva Strachan said for me to —" She broke off, her eyes roaming the crowded room desperately.

"Kincardine!" Jeneva said, pushing back her chair and rising with what seemed to be genuine delight. "Kincardine, my dear. How lovely to have you here." She pushed an offending corner of the table out of the way and swept forward in a waft of expensive perfume. "Everyone, this is

Kincardine O'Neil. She's assisting us, this production. Kincardine, this is...well, you'll meet everyone when we have more time. You're here just in the nick, darling, we're absolutely into this scene, and it's going so well, maybe you won't mind just waiting for a bit, just till the next natural stopping place. All right? No, darling, not that wall, we'll be using that in a moment. Can't you just find a quiet perch somewhere you won't be in the way, there's a good girl."

Lucas had no reason to like this Kincardine O'Neil, but there was something so dignified about the way she got herself over to the opposite wall, found a stool, and sat down, very straight, that caught his sympathy. He went behind the backdrop and retrieved the girl's suitcase from near the fire door, returned the same way, and put it at her feet.

"Thank you," she said, not looking at him.

It was not exactly an invitation to stay, but he had nothing to do in this scene, and there was another free stool nearby. He pulled it a little closer to her and sat down.

The scene had switched again. Macbeth and his friend Banquo were on stage, asking the three witches how far it was to Forres. When one of the witches told Macbeth he was destined to become king of Scotland, Lucas watched Alexander Blair critically. Blair was obviously used to the role of Macbeth but there was something wrong with his interpretation of the character. Blair was making Macbeth too evil, too greedy for kingship.

"He wasn't like that," Lucas muttered to himself, and was surprised when the girl, answered him.

"Mac — the Thane wasn't, you mean? What *was* he like then?"

"Trapped," Lucas surprised himself by saying.

"Quiet in the wings!" thundered the God Incarnate.

When it was time for Macbeth to go off by himself and give his speech about what the witches' prophecy meant to him, Jeneva stopped the scene. "Again, from the top," she called, from her table. "Try it from farther back, over near the door. Forget the rest of us. Talk only to each other."

The three witches moved into the corner near the fire door. Lucas chewed his lip, watching. There was something different about that corner, something that hadn't been there when he'd gone over to get the girl's suitcase. Something thin as a hair from this distance, but so shiny its copper colour caught the light and winked at him. He didn't know what it was, but he knew it shouldn't be there, hanging just where Joan Mackenzie was going to walk into it when she stepped forward to greet Macbeth.

A humped, dark shadow moved briefly into his line of sight, and out again. Lucas's heart beat harder. The copper-coloured thing glittered. Lucas got off his stool. Wire. It was wire. Uninsulated. But surely not live?

Macbeth and Banquo entered, saw the three witches, asked about Forres. Joan Mackenzie stepped forward. She saw the hanging wire in her way; it was only natural for her to try to push it away.

"No!" Lucas shouted – too late.

A flash! A terrible sizzle, a smell, screaming; and rattling, rattling, teeth and bones too; hair standing on end, no way to stop it, wire fused to hand and skin to wire and no way to stop it, someone shouting sensible things, throw the main switch, get a doctor; but it all took too long, and still Joan shook and shook. And when, at last, the power went off, no one could be sure what happened, not till their eyes got used to the sudden dark. But Lucas thought he saw a humped shadow walk by him, out into the corridor and away. Then someone opened the fire door, and they could all see what was left of Joan Mackenzie, lying on the floor, shapeless as a rag in the afternoon sunlight with its golden dustmotes drifting all around.

Chapter Four

"I T'S THIS PLAY," CHRISTINE GALE PROJECTED tearfully. "It's cursed, poor Joan. It's this awful, awful play!"

A wild-haired young man sitting across the table from Kinny leaned over to pass Christine a paper napkin. "Your mascara's running," he said.

Kinny looked at him dully. It was the actor she'd yelled at this afternoon at the stage door. The sarcastic one. Adam. She turned her head. The other two men who'd been at the stage door were here, too. The guy with the sexy voice. What was his name? Something arty. Norris, that was it. He was sitting beside her. And Lucas was at the end of the table. She remembered him, all right. He was the one who had got her suitcase for her when she'd been so stupid about coming into the hall while a scene was being rehearsed. He was the one she'd accused of abandoning his French-Canadian ancestry.

Why was she with these people? It had something to do with Lucas, Kinny remembered that much. She'd been in the rehearsal hall, and Joan Mackenzie had...there had been that terrible...and then, somehow, she was here with Lucas standing over her holding a mug of very sweet coffee to her lips and telling her she had to drink it and calling her Kincardine. "My name's Kinny," she'd corrected him and tried to push the coffee away, but he insisted, and it was easier to obey.

The room was the big, cheerful cafeteria known as the Green Room. It was painted dull green, but that wasn't why it was called that. Kinny knew all theatres had a Green Room where actors and backstage staff gathered to relax. But here the atmosphere was anything but relaxed. Joan Mackenzie was dead, electrocuted by a high voltage wire that had somehow worked its way loose from its connection.

"I don't know why anybody ever tries to produce the Scottish play," Norris said broodingly. "It always means accidents."

"They were cleaning the light fixtures last night," said Adam. "I heard that one of the ladders caught in a wire and pulled it loose. The custodians wouldn't have noticed. Only one end was live, and you could hardly see it, dangling there."

"There wasn't any wire dangling when I got Kinny's suitcase," Lucas said, "and that was just before it happened."

"Are you sure, Lucas?" Christine said, her round eyes big.

"Well," Norris said, "a ladder could have loosened the wire, without making it fall right away. Maybe it was hanging by a thread, and then a truck went by just before Joan —"

"Or vibrations from the actors' voices —"

"That's right, they were right underneath. Maybe —"

They were all talking at once, all except Lucas, Kinny noticed. And me, too, she thought. She still felt unsteady, even sitting here with both elbows on a solid table, both hands around a thick mug, both feet on ordinary red linoleum. Until today Kinny had never seen anyone die.

After that everything had gone dark. People explained the darkness, later. The master switch had to be thrown to cut off the power before anyone could touch Joan, or help her. It would have been too late to do anything useful anyway, people said. She had died instantly; all that shaking and burning and that horrible, horrible smell had happened to a corpse, not a living person. Joan wouldn't have felt it. That's what they said.

But Kinny's darkness continued for a long time after the lights went back on.

Sometime, in the dark, there had been eyes looking at her. It was the only clear thing in all the blackness, that pair of eyes gleaming pale and cold. Ruthless eyes, they were, desperate eyes that had been looking for something for a long time and were too near to finding it to let anything interfere. They sharpened into a kind of alarmed speculation when they got to Kinny, and for a long shocked moment she felt as if she were in the principal's office at school being raked over the coals for some major transgression. She didn't remember anything after that, not until that first sip of too-sweet coffee.

"– and I heard that Joan's understudy quit and Jeneva was already on the phone for a replacement before they got the body out of there."

"They're not going to cancel the show, then?" Norris asked, sounding relieved.

Adam threw him a look, deeply sardonic. "'The show must go on.' 'It's what Joan would have wanted.' Can't you just hear the platitudes? Of course they're not going to cancel it! It'd cost too much."

"But no one will want to work on the production, now!" Christine exclaimed. "Look at Joan's understudy...everyone'll be as scared as she is."

"But not everyone's as stupid. Take you, Chrissie. Your first big break at Stratford, and a European tour at the end of it. Are you really going to walk out on all that? When Jeneva's sure to tell all future directors the names of the actors who let her down on this show?"

Dead silence.

"Who's Jeneva getting for First Witch?" Lucas said, after a moment.

"Some unknown, probably," Norris said. "The biggies are already taken."

"It's not that important a role, really," Adam said, shrugging. "Anybody would do."

"What do you know about it?" Christine flared. "You've only got one real scene. The witches have three, and they're important, not like *your* cowardly little bit part!"

"You don't have to get personal. I just said it wasn't a big enough role to need somebody with a name."

"I've got to go," Norris said, pushing back his chair.

"It's always the same at Stratford," Christine said bitterly as Norris walked away. "Never enough parts for the women, and when you do finally get a decent one, the men sneer at you." She turned to Kinny, adding dramatically, "Don't ever become an actress, darling."

Adam gave a nasty laugh. "If you ever become one, Chrissie, maybe people like Kinny will listen to your advice about it."

Christine gave an outraged gasp. Kinny looked into her coffee cup. "Better drink the rest," Lucas advised her, as calmly as if nothing else were happening. "You're still pretty white."

"It's cold," Kinny whispered.

"You can reheat it. There's a microwave." He pointed. He was being kind, but his concern felt completely impersonal to Kinny. She could imagine him doing the same for anybody.

Christine was on her feet. "Curtain at the Avon in an hour. I've got to run. Goodbye, Lucas. Welcome to Stratford, Kinny." She swept regally away, seeming unaware of the irony in her last words, or of Adam sitting there chortling.

"Why don't you leave people alone, Adam?" Lucas said, as if he really wanted to know.

"My duty as an actor," he replied smugly. "Gotta find out what makes the hoi polloi tick. Anyway, you don't need to worry about Chrissie. She's too lazy to hold a grudge." He grimaced at the dirty dishes she'd left behind her. "Greedy little pig, too. Did you ever see anybody eat cake and cry at the same time? And her on a diet."

"It's not to lose weight," Lucas said wearily, "she's a borderline diabetic. She needs to eat when she's had a shock."

Adam leered at Kinny. "What about you, sweetcheeks? You didn't eat a thing."

"I'm not hungry."

"Can't have that. You want to be healthy if you're going to work for Jeneva."

"I never get sick," Kinny said.

"So *are* you working for Jeneva, or the Festival?"

"Jeneva, I think," she answered warily.

"You think? What does that mean?"

"It means the only play I'm working on is hers. The Scottish play."

"Will you be going on tour with us?"

"Just the first part of the tour. Edinburgh, not Munich or any of the other places." She wouldn't tell him that Dad was paying her way to Scotland and back.

"You've got a place to stay while you're here, I hope. Stratford's always jammed in the summer."

"I'm in a bed-and-breakfast," she said. She got her purse out, looked at a sheet of paper, and said, "'Granny's Attic,' it's called."

"Over on Water Street? That's a good location. You must have connections, kid." He gave her a curious look.

"Don't push it, Adam," Lucas murmured.

"Push it?" Adam raised his eyes, innocent as a baby. "Me?"

"It's getting late," Kinny said abruptly. "I should go."

"Do you want a lift over to Water Street?" Adam asked. "I've got a car, and that looks like a heavy suitcase."

"No thanks," she said quickly. "The brochure said it wasn't far from the theatre. And I like walking."

"So I can't corner you to find out how you

managed to wangle a good B&B, to say nothing of a job working for Jeneva?"

"I'm sure you have bigger hoi polloi to fry," she said.

He snorted with laughter. "Obviously you're feeling better," he said. "You'll be taking up arms for the French again before we know it."

He left almost at once. Kinny felt very tired. She wanted to go, but she simply didn't have the energy to get up. Lucas sat there, sipping coffee and looking abstracted, as if he were thinking hard.

"Did you see an old woman in the rehearsal hall?" he demanded suddenly. "Humpbacked, white braid, really strange eyes?"

Kinny had started to shake her head, but the last part stopped her.

"What do you mean, strange? Their colour?"

"Silver, almost. And they shone. They —" He broke off.

"What are you getting at?"

He began stirring his coffee. "I don't know. Everyone liked Joan. It must have been an accident, but still...."

Kinny realized suddenly what Lucas was thinking. "Nobody could have known it would be Joan who'd get electrocuted by the wire," she said horrified. "Anybody could have —"

"Not anybody." He stared into his coffee. "It would have to have been one of the witches.

That was their corner. The wire came loose after Jeneva told the witches to go over there."

"You don't think *Jeneva* —" Kinny said, shocked.

"Of course not. She was at her table the whole time."

"That old woman, then. The humpback with the strange eyes. You think she did something, don't you?"

"She was there," he said. "I saw her in that corner. At least, I think I did. But nobody else seems to have noticed her in the room at all, so maybe I'm crazy."

But it was even crazier to see only a pair of eyes, and no body to go with them. And to imagine that those eyes were asking her things...Lucas would laugh at her if she told him that. Kinny sat silent, feeling suddenly very alone.

All her excitement at coming to Stratford was gone. She remembered her embarrassing entrance to the rehearsal hall, and the way Jeneva had sent her to a stool, saying, "There's a good girl." Jeneva hadn't wanted her at the rehearsal, that was clear. Jeneva didn't want her at Stratford at all. Funny how, in all her own thinking about Mom getting her this job, it hadn't occurred to Kinny to wonder how Jeneva would feel about it. And then that whole awful time sitting there on that stool while the rehearsal went on, thinking about how Jeneva felt, only now and then watching, only now and then letting her attention be caught by the play.

And then Lucas jumping up and yelling, and a woman dying, and that darkness, and those eyes.

Lucas picked up Kinny's coffee cup, went over to the microwave, heated the coffee, and brought it back for her. "Drink it," he ordered.

She surprised herself by obeying.

"I'm walking right by your B&B," Lucas said, when she was done. "I'll take you over there, if you like."

Again that kindness, impersonal as before. As he picked up her suitcase, the isolated, abstracted expression returned to his face. He led the way through the maze of corridors and down the staircase to the stage door. The door-man waved to her, and she was glad of that, because she had been feeling invisible, with Lucas so silent. But she didn't mind his silence as they walked to her B&B in the golden sum-mer evening. She was just grateful that he was there. Because all the way, right up to the moment he handed her her suitcase at the front door, Kinny felt as if another pair of eyes were on her, and they were cold eyes, and pale, and they wished she were alone.

PIPES CLANGING. The hiss of hot water in the bathroom next door. Singing, tentative at first, then louder, and increasingly out-of-tune. "And the night/has a thousand eyes...."

Stretching in the morning light, Kinny smiled to herself. There had been no eyes in the night for her. Any eyes that might have wanted to get into one of Mrs. Emma Palfrey's pink-and-white bedrooms in the middle of the night would have had a hard job. Mrs. Palfrey had run Granny's Attic as a bed and breakfast for at least fifteen years, and though she'd never been robbed, she was sure that one day she would be. She told Kinny that within five minutes of meeting her, handing her the three different keys required to open the front door.

"Don't lose them, dear, and don't let anybody else get hold of them," she had said firmly. "People will be people, and there's no point in encouraging the bad ones."

All the windows, even the ones far above ground level, were covered with ornate ironwork on the inside of the frame, so that the windows could be safely cranked open. There were three guest bedrooms on the third floor, and they all had a fireplace with a cast-iron screen that could be locked in place for extra security. Kinny had the room in the middle. With the bedside lamp off and no moon and only the streetlamp to cast any shadows, she had looked out through the decorative iron to the quiet street lined with trees and big old houses. It was empty even of cars. The only noise was the faint rustling of trees. Kinny had run her fingers over the protective iron curtain. Then she climbed under the sheets and slept at once.

At breakfast, the owner of the voice in the shower turned out to be a lighting designer for the Festival. His name was Andrew Vance.

"Assistant to the assistant for *Hamlet*," he said. "They let me change a lightbulb, now and then. What about you?"

Kinny put down her toast. "I'm doing less than that," she said, trying to smile. "I'm just, well, helping out, I guess. Only one production. *Macb—*" She stopped herself in time. "The Scottish play, I mean."

His pug-dog face went grave. "That was terrible, yesterday. You were there? Grim." He gave her a sympathetic nod. "But accidents happen, you can't expect them not to, with this many people doing technical things in one small place. They're going on with rehearsals in the hall just as soon as the police are finished with their investigation —"

"The police?"

"— and I think that's smart. No sense giving people time to develop phobias about Rehearsal Hall 3."

Of course there would be a police investigation, Kinny told herself. A sudden death; people had to find out why the accident had happened. Accident....

It was a perfect summer morning. The swans were out on the river, and people were already draped over the railings of a little arched bridge that led to a island. The whole riverside was a garden, a riot of purple and pink. Kinny tried to remember her euphoria yesterday after lunch, walking from the train station for the first time and seeing the famous tent-like roof of the Festival Theatre come into view. It seemed like another life.

At the stage door, someone else was on duty, not her friend of the day before, and there was a huge sign posted below his cage. "MACB. rehearsals cancelled for today. Full cast call, 10:00 a.m. tomorrow."

Kinny read it, and hesitated.

"Yes?" said the doorman.

"I'm Kinny O'Neil," she said, adding automatically, "Kincardine O'Neil, really. Did Jeneva Strachan leave a message for me?"

The guard checked his papers.

"Nothing here," he said after a minute.

"Is Jeneva in?"

"She's busy all day. She's asked not to be disturbed."

Yesterday, Kinny would have argued. Today she only nodded, went back out the door, and headed for the river. Definitely not wanted.

There was no one around, no one close, just a few tourists ogling swans on the riverbank and one white-haired woman with her back to Kinny. But someone was looking at her. Kinny checked over her shoulder, then scanned the river-bank again. No one. She wriggled her shoulders, but the odd sensation, annoying as an itch, wouldn't go away. There were eyes on her, she was sure of it.

She hurried away from the river, bought herself some bread and juice and cheese at a deli and a small paring knife and a plastic plate at Woolco, then headed back toward Mrs. Palfrey and her triple-locked doors and iron-curtained windows. The eyes, clear and cold, went with her all the way to the steps leading up to the old-fashioned front door. There, suddenly, they went away.

Seeing me home, Kinny thought. Or had she imagined the whole thing? She used her three keys, and went up to her room. There she alternated between reading and thinking until it was time for bread and cheese and another night's sleep.

❈ ❈ ❈

JUST BEFORE TEN the next morning Kinny made her way into Rehearsal Hall 3 behind the rolling bulk of Everett Lunn. She felt nervous, going back into the place where Joan Mackenzie had been killed. Her eyes went first to the corner by the fire door. The spot where Joan had died was empty of people, and that stood out, because the rest of the hall was crowded. It would have stood out anyway, because one of the high-tech cue-lights from under the balcony had been turned on and its intense white beam was aimed directly at the spot where Joan had fallen. The rest of the hall was rather dim. Kinny wondered if the place where Joan had died had been lit up like that as a kind of tribute. But there was nothing else to indicate that, nothing out of the ordinary at all. Not even any police chalk-marks on the floor. She looked up. There were no hanging wires. She had known there wouldn't be, but she had had to check just the same.

The hall was very quiet, considering that so many people were there. The cast seemed outnumbered by publicity people and front-of-house staff and producers and personnel officers, all of them smiling a lot – wide, determined smiles, denying that anything could possibly be wrong. The actors stood in small, defensive huddles, drinking coffee, murmuring.

Jeneva was over by her table, leafing through some notes. She was wearing a long white caftan. A single silver earring dangled its crescent almost to her shoulder. For once she was alone. Kinny squared her shoulders and marched over.

"Morning, Jeneva," she said. Too soft. She cleared her throat. "Jeneva?"

The director looked up. "Oh, yes, Kinny." Her face was closed, the bones sharp as beaks. She waited. Her eyes grew impatient. "Yes?"

"I was wondering — that is, I don't know what you want me to — what my job —" Kinny stammered to a halt.

"Your job?" She frowned.

"I'm here to work," Kinny said, and to her shame added, "aren't I?"

Jeneva rubbed her chin with a long, elegant index finger. "Of course you are, Kinny," she said. "The thing is, you can't do very much that's useful until you can find your way around. Why don't you spend the first few days getting to know people, figuring out where everything is, that sort of thing? I'll tell everyone to take some time to explain things." Her eyes were already straying back to her notes. Something in Kinny's silence must have alerted her; she looked up again and said, "We'll talk job description next week, darling, I promise. Okay?" She looked over Kinny's head, and called, "Ready, Everett."

Everett Lunn rapped sharply on the table. "Will you turn your eyes this way, ladies and gentlemen, please. Jeneva has something important to say."

Chapter Five

J ENEVA TURNED AWAY FROM HER NOTES AND walked out onto the practice stage. Slowly, serenely, she headed for the brightly lit corner near the fire door. The cast stirred uneasily. She was now on the exact spot where Joan had met her end, not quite two days before.

For a long time Jeneva only stood there, her back to them. Her body cast strange shadows on the spotlit floor. In her white caftan she looked like a priestess, head bowed, hands invisible but presumably clasped in front of her.

"Good staging," Adam murmured.

Lucas blinked. Adam was right. It *was* staging, done for effect, but the odd thing was that even here, even in front of an audience of people who knew all about the technicalities of lighting and costume and gesture, it was effective. People were watching Jeneva with barely a sound. It was because of where she was standing, Lucas suddenly realized. No one in the superstitious theatre community would have chosen to stand in a place one of them had died only two days before except as an honest tribute to the dead person. The fact that Jeneva was using all her art to pay tribute to Joan Mackenzie did not diminish that tribute at all.

Slowly Jeneva turned. Her caftan shifted gently; shadows swirled beneath her. She faced her audience. "Joan was a wonderful woman," she said, "an intelligent woman, a woman with a deep understanding of the playwright's craft. When I first asked her to be one of our witches, do you know what she said? She said she had been thinking of taking up an offer from the Shaw Festival this summer instead of coming back to Stratford, but that a role in the Scottish play changed everything. She said it was her favourite play, a marvellous play. She was right. It is a marvellous play."

"Not so marvellous for Joan," Adam whispered to Lucas, who shifted away slightly. He had no desire to be Adam's confidant.

"This isn't the time for dramaturgy," Jeneva continued, "but the central idea of the play has something vital to say about what happened in this room, on this very spot, two days ago. And so I want to talk about it now." She sent a thoughtful, almost gentle look around the hall, seeming to spend a little extra time on Adam.

"The Scottish play isn't just about a man who kills a king and takes his place," Jeneva went on. "It isn't even solely about his motivation – his ambition, his fascination with witchcraft, his dark love for the wife who persuades him to murder King Duncan. I think this is a play about power. Power. Who has it, who wants it, who takes it, who abuses it. And who is defeated by it."

She paused, letting her words sink in. No one said anything. No one even moved. She nodded, abruptly. Change of pace, Lucas thought. Here we go.

"Troublesome things have happened in other productions of this play. A dreadfully troublesome thing has happened in our own. Joan —" Her breath caught. She shook her head. "No, I won't talk any more about her now — there will be a better time for all of us to show our deep respect and love for her — but I have to say one thing about her death, because it affects how we are all going to carry on after today. You will know by now that the police have found Joan's death to be an accident."

She threw her head back. Her voice grew richer, and very even. "But there have been lots of accidents in the history of this play, haven't there? We all know it. We're all thinking about it. And what we're wondering is this — Was Joan's death just an ordinary accident, or was it an accident caused by the fact that we're producing what some people call a bad-luck play? In other words, do we superstitious actors ascribe Joan's accident to some power in the Scottish play to control her life and her death, or do we refuse to allow it that power?"

Her voice strengthened. She seemed to be growing by the moment, taller and brighter and more elegant and more in charge with every word she spoke. Lucas watched her with fascination. Whether she was right that power was what the Scottish play was all about, there was one thing for sure – it was what Jeneva Strachan was all about. She came alive just using the word.

"Now this is what I think. This play has a bad luck reputation, yes. But it's got that reputation because a few unlucky things happened during its earliest productions, and a few superstitious people made a point of recording them. Then later productions were observed to see if more unlucky events occurred. Once people looked for disaster they got it, because people who are frightened, people who expect danger to leap out at them at the slightest opportunity, are people who overreact to small perils and so create large ones. In other words, the only power the play has ever had to cause accidents was given to it by the people who expected it to have that kind of power."

She looked magnificent, shining in her circle of high-intensity white light. Even Adam seemed to have lost his cynical expression.

"What do we conclude from all this? I'll tell you what *I* conclude. This play, this marvellous play, has power to cause us harm only if we allow it that power. And *I* won't allow it. I refuse to allow it. I know, you see, that I'm much more powerful than the play, and so are you."

She smiled brilliantly. "Modest? Of course not. But I can cancel the play, if I choose; I can change it; I can drop scenes; I can make it say something about Canada when the playwright barely knew such a place existed. I'm not under the play's control, and neither are any of you. On the contrary, we control it." Her voice changed again, growing almost intimate.

"Joan's accident was just that, my dears. An accident can happen on any set, in any play. It has nothing to do with this play's bad luck history. All we have to do is believe that, and take regular ordinary care, and we will be completely safe from future harm. I assure you I am right. Let's get on with why we're here. Let's get on with this marvellous, marvellous play."

A power struggle between the actors and the play! It caught everyone's imagination. People were visibly relaxing, nodding, moving in closer to Jeneva. She was leaving the stage now, making her way through the crowd, chatting and smiling, exchanging nods with Alexander Blair, patting Christine on the shoulder, hugging someone else. "A real love-in," Lucas said to himself. He must have said it aloud, because Adam grinned appreciatively.

"Clear the stage!" Everett Lunn called, as if on cue. "Miss Archer, Meredith Archer, please! Act One, Scene 5, enter Lady Macbeth with letter."

Everyone but Meredith Archer, as Lady Macbeth, left the practice stage. Someone handed her a sheet of paper. She cleared her throat, held the paper up before her, and pretended to read from it. She stopped reading. She held the letter to her breast. She spoke the words Shakespeare had given her, and no one hearing her could have imagined that Macbeth could escape this woman's will.

She's good, Lucas thought. She's really good.

The messenger came and went. Macbeth came in. He spoke with his Lady. King Duncan was coming to stay with them tonight, and would leave tomorrow. Lady Macbeth's ominous reply — "Oh never shall sun that morrow see!"— made Lucas's eyes shine. This was acting!

"Back to the top," Jeneva said, interrupting near the end. "More sex when Alex comes in, Meredith, please. He's your husband, he's been at war, you know what he likes. Give it to him. Only a taste, mind, just enough to keep him hungry. Because that's the source of your power over him. And you need that power, remember. You're going to have to make him kill his king."

They started over. Alexander Blair came in.

Meredith threw down the letter and ran to him, crying, "I feel now the future in the instant!"

And at that same instant, the fire door opened, and a woman stepped in. "I'm told," she said into the suddenly silent hall, "that someone here is looking for a witch."

🈁 🈁 🈁

She was an unusual-looking woman. Even without that entrance of hers she would have attracted attention. She was fifty, maybe, or even older, with smooth apple cheeks as round as a girl's, an innocent mouth that looked as if it had never worn lipstick, a crêpe paper neck, and wide open blue eyes that seemed to shine with astonishment. She wore her silver-blond hair long, and the smooth peekaboo style didn't suit her flowery muslin dress with its high neck and long sleeves. She wasn't abnormally tall, but the dress was a little too short for her. It made Lucas think of skinned knees, ankle socks, and patent leather shoes.

Jeneva swept to her side. "You must be Dana Sloe. How wonderful that you could get here so soon. Alex, Meredith, all of you, meet Dana Sloe, our new First Witch. She's played the role all over the U.K., and we're very lucky she happened to be visiting a friend here in Canada and agreed to help us out.

The company murmured their greetings.

"Welcome to the company, Dana," Everett said. "We're doing the Letter Scene. Why don't you have a seat? Or maybe you want to find a hotel right away and get settled."

"I'd like to watch," Dana Sloe said. Lucas was surprised at the authority in her voice. It didn't seem to go with the rest of her at all. "I already have a place to stay."

Jeneva led her to a chair near where Lucas was sitting. While Everett dusted it off ostentatiously, Dana Sloe smiled at Lucas. It was a sweet, gentle smile, but he returned it only perfunctorily, more interested in her eyes. They were as opaque as a pair of mirrors. Close up they weren't blue at all, but almost silver.

"Dana Sloe," Adam said brightly to the newcomer. "Slow with a W, or with an E?"

"Which would you prefer?" she replied coolly. "You can make a decent joke out of either."

"I don't think I —"

"Gin, dear. Sloe gin. A lovely liqueur made of the fruit of the blackthorn tree. I'm sure you can carry the ball from there." She had Adam pegged, all right. Lucas had seldom seen the other man so disconcerted. Again he looked at her shiny, unrevealing eyes. He'd been wrong about her voice not belonging with the rest of her. It exactly suited those eyes.

He saw Kinny hovering nearby. Little girl

lost, Lucas thought. He found himself going over to her.

"You okay?" he said. "Jeneva keeping you busy?"

She smiled brilliantly. "Meredith Archer is wonderful, isn't she?"

He pitied her suddenly. "She certainly is," he said. "Come and have a coffee with me."

"Get one for Dana, will you, Kinny?" Jeneva called as they headed for the large coffee urn set up near the hall door.

Kinny's lips tightened, but she nodded.

"You handling the French business all right with Jeneva?"

"What?" She looked bewildered.

"You know, her interpretation of the play. You had some pretty strong ideas about the French-English situation in Quebec, I seem to recall."

"I still do. And I think a French-Canadian *Macbe* — Scottish play, I mean —"

"French-Canadian-Scottish play," Lucas murmured. "Sounds like the United Nations."

"Anyway, it's just what we don't need in this country. We've got enough anti-French bigots without somebody like Jeneva making one of the biggest bad guys in the theatre into the French general who lost Quebec. If Jeneva thought about it, she'd —" She stopped, looking miserable. "I can't even tell her what I think. I was supposed to come here as her assistant, but instead, I pour coffee."

So that was what was wrong. Lucas said carefully, "You can't have had very much back-stage experience. Maybe Jeneva wants to give you time to get to know Stratford before...."

"That's what she said." Again that brilliant smile. "So I thought I'd go down to Wardrobe. See if I can help out making costumes."

They were very busy in Wardrobe at this time of the season. Lucas remembered Doris's impatience when Adam had teased her the other day. The last thing they would want would be a kid coming in and trying to help, when they could do everything better and faster on their own. Somehow Lucas didn't want Kinny to get the rough side of Doris's tongue. He drank down his coffee, trying to think of some way to tell her without hurting her feel-ings.

"You think I'll be in the way, don't you?" Kinny said, adding defensively, "I helped sew costumes for all my school shows."

School shows weren't Stratford, Lucas thought.

Kinny was watching him. She sighed. "Would I be in the way in Props, too?"

So she was smart. And she knew how to back down. However she'd gotten this so-called job working for Jeneva, she deserved better than she was getting. He put down his cup. "There are always more jobs to do in Props than there are people to do them," he said. "I know the man in charge down there. Jim'll be pleased to meet you. Why don't we go now, before the break is over?"

Kinny looked at him gratefully. "Just let me get rid of this coffee."

JIM SIMPSON WAS A COMPACT, spidery-looking man with what seemed to be more than the usual number of limbs, a gruff voice, and friendly eyes. "You bet we can use you," he told Kinny, when Lucas had introduced them. "For instance, sewing maple leaves. Grand total of 21,500 needed for that tree for *Macbeth* —" He broke off, seeing her flinch. "Don't you like sewing?"

"It's not that," Kinny said quickly. "It's just that you called the Scottish play —"

"*Macbeth*," Jim repeated cheerfully. "I'm not an actor, thank God. I'd never remember all the things I'm not supposed to do. *Macbeth*, *Macbeth*, *Macbeth*. See, I'm still alive. Want to try it? Take some of the wind out of superstition's sails. No? Rather sew instead, would you? Good enough." He took a breath, but before she could say anything he was off again. "Five pair of hands in this place — now six, thanks to you,

Lucas, and of course thanks to the lovebug here – and a million things to do besides sewing leaves. Whose idea was it to have a perfectly beautiful Canadian maple in the middle of the *Macbeth* set, anyway?"

"I'll leave you to it," Lucas said.

Kinny smiled at him, feeling a bit out-of-breath but happier than she'd been in two days. When he had disappeared through the door she followed Jim to a wide bench along one of the walls. The room was very large and had hardly any furnishings of its own. It didn't look plain, though. Stage furniture in all stages of construction littered every surface – onyx-like tables, chairs whose legs looked like gargoyles, a large sedan chair, urns big enough to hold a body, stacks and stacks of armour – "We turn breast-plates out by the hundreds," Jim said complacently – oil lamps in sconces, a whole banquet of fibreglass foods. There was simply too much to take in all at once.

Jim was waiting for her at the bench, where there were two cartons full of maple leaves. "You'll be working on your own for a while," he said. "There always seems to be another job more pressing to do when I ask somebody to work on these." He pulled a handful of leaves out of a carton and showed them to her. "Real-looking aren't they?" he said happily. "Six different patterns, six different colours of red, all the veins soldered in by hand, none of the painted junk you'd see in Toronto. We sew on wires for stems and tape them with florist's tape to larger wire branches which we'll attach to the steel tubing tree trunk you may have seen out at the end of the hall. That trunk's been designed to fit around one of the pillars on the stage upstairs, the central one supporting the balcony. Whole thing will take thousands of hours, but it'll last forever, and there won't be one person in the audience who won't think it's real."

He put her to work sewing stems onto the pre-cut leaves. At first she gave it all her concentration, but after a dozen leaves she had gotten the hang of it, and could look around while she sewed. Jim came and went, giving instructions to his staff, lending a hand where needed, throwing a cheerful word to Kinny now and then, but most often just tinkering with the vacuum form machine that was, he said, his favourite toy. Kinny hadn't quite figured out what it did, something to do with fibreglass and moulds for things like armour that needed to be mass produced, but she didn't like machines much anyway. The blue and green styrofoam cubes were far more interesting to her. They were the miracles of deception in any Props Department, Jim said. As an illustration he lifted with one hand an entire fireplace that

Kinny would have sworn was made of marble, then tossed it to his other hand. "Styrofoam," he said, grinning. "It's wonderful stuff. You can carve it and you can paint it, and from five feet away, if you do it right, people swear it's the real thing."

Kinny ate lunch in the Green Room with Jean, another woman who worked in the Props Department. She was about five years older than Kinny, fair-haired and tiny and with amazing biceps, and after only a few minutes in her company Kinny knew that she was a worrier. She worried about finding a place to sit in the Green Room, and she worried about how much time it would take to get their order ready; she spent most of the lunch break worrying about her car, the silverfish in her apartment, and whether she'd ever have time to finish the hand-mirror she was making.

"You just don't know the trouble I've had with that mirror," she said, while they were having their coffee. "Every time I think I've got it right something happens. Today it was the metallic paint. I don't know what went wrong. It was supposed to go on smooth, but instead the whole thing wrinkled. I'm going to have to start over. *Again.*"

"Don't you ever buy your props?" Kinny said. "I mean, mirrors are so common. Why waste your time making one?"

"This is no ordinary mirror. It's supposed to look magical."

"What play's it in?"

"The Scottish play." Clearly Jean didn't share Jim's approach to the superstitions about *Macbeth*. "Probably that's why the damn thing won't let itself get made. The play's put a curse on it."

"I don't remember any mirror in the Scottish play."

"Of course you don't. No one does. It's only there for about ten seconds. It's near the end. Remember where the witches call up a lot of demon apparitions to answer the big M's questions?"

"Wait a minute. I do remember. *Show his eyes and grieve his heart. Come like shadows, so depart.*"

"I wish you hadn't done that," Jean said plaintively.

"What?"

"Quoted from...that play. It's unlucky."

Kinny chewed her lip. Another bad luck rule she'd forgotten. She had a quick mental flash of the only production of *Macbeth* she had ever seen, the witches watching their cauldron sink as if by magic into the earthen stage, all that smoke and cackling and Macbeth staring at them in horror and greed while they croaked out those very words she'd just quoted. And then the dead Banquo appearing, showing his

d Montcalm was an out-and-out mur-
Alex demanded skeptically.

t of people died on the Plains of Abra-
neva said.

ought it was the English who attacked
ich, there. Surely Montcalm was just
g his territory —"

French have always believed the best
s offense," Jeneva said. "It's still going
how they've kicked out the English
munity to protect their own. There's
nt English-language theatre left in all
lid you know? Fifteen years ago there
ist a dozen."

e said anything. Everyone knew that
done her most important work at
Saidye Bronfman Theatre before
t cutbacks in funding and declining
rale had shut it down. There had
g for her in Quebec since, especially
d been interviewed on national tele-
sting the province's funding poli-

artists from doing their work is a
der," Jeneva said. "There are other
urder of language is one. And if
rates from the rest of Canada,
der too. A whole country, killed."
nch in Quebec could say that
Plains of Abraham killed *their*

bloody wounds to Macbeth, the man responsible for his murder. And all those descendants of Banquo's coming after him, eight kings in a line and the eighth carrying a mirror which showed Macbeth many more. And how Macbeth felt about it, knowing that he'd killed Banquo to prevent him from fathering kings, and knowing, now, how useless it had all been.

Jean was already on to a new worry. Or rather, to the same old one. "It's got to look old as well as magical," she was saying.

The mirror, again. "Antique stores," Kinny suggested.

"I know. But Jeneva's such a stickler. She knows exactly what she wants. The decorations at the side...."

"So buy an antique mirror and decorate it. It's the glass you're having trouble with, you said. So buy the glass, and do what you want with it."

Jean stared. "That's a good idea, Kinny. A really good idea. I don't think Jim would mind. He's getting sick of me working on the thing, with all those maple leaves to deal with."

"Speaking of which," Kinny said, looking at her watch.

"Come shopping with me after work," Jean urged, as they hurried back downstairs. "We'll see if we can find the right kind of mirror. No point in talking to Jim about it till we know there is one."

Entering the Props Department, Jim greeted them with a cheerful torrent of inconsequential talk. A few of the other members of the department nodded in a friendly way. Kinny went back to her sewing. For the first time since arriving at Stratford, she felt as if she belonged.

But still, she wished she hadn't quoted that line from the Scottish play.

Chapte

"THANK YOU, LAD Jeneva said. "Y ful."

She sounded as fresh ning of the day instea hours of intense rehea either, but he could s else was. Alexander famous blue eyes had the bags beneath th etched around his n Alex's acting today. S what he was doir Macbeth just bef Duncan.

"If there's one wishy-washy," Jene

"It *is* written killing Duncan replied, bridling.

"Of course i right. But we are I mean, Genera But in this pro as much as you

---

"An derer?"

"A l ham," J

"I th the Frei defendir

"The defense i on. Lool arts com one decer Quebec, were at le

No on Jeneva ha Montreal's governmen English m been nothir after she ha vision prot cies.

"To stop kind of mu kinds. The Quebec sep that'll be mu

"The Fre battle on the

country," Alex pointed out.

"And the Scots might say that the final battle between Malcolm and our Thane killed theirs," Jeneva agreed with surprising calm. "After Malcolm took over, the ruling power in Scotland became English, the same way it did in Quebec after the Plains of Abraham. That parallel is one reason our setting for the play works so well. The Scots are even thinking of separating from the United Kingdom the same way Quebec is from Canada. For the Scots it all goes back to the conflict between Malcolm and the Big M, the same way our Canadian problems all go back to the Plains of Abraham." She looked down at her notes and added evenly, "Can we try the Dagger Scene again now?"

The historical parallels were all very well, Lucas thought, but on their own they weren't enough to make Jeneva's ideas for this play succeed. A year ago he himself had been in a terrific modern-dress *King Lear* set in the Southern U.S., and once on TV he'd seen a *Henry V* set during the First World War. Both of these had been exciting non-traditional productions that used the plays' truths to make statements about their unusual settings. But Jeneva was trying to do it the other way around. She had her own statement to make, and she was trying to mould the play to fit it. And the statement she was making didn't sit comfortably with Lucas.

He wasn't French-Canadian, he was American, he had no personal stake in the matter. But Jeneva was using his favourite play to say that Canada could only be put right if the French were put down, and that made him feel uneasy.

And the important things, like Macbeth's true character, were getting left out. Alex was trying to work on it, but Jeneva wouldn't let him. The Dagger Scene was a complex one and Lucas wasn't sure how it should be played, but he was positive it wasn't the way Jeneva insisted. He longed to be up there on the practice stage in Alex's place, with the freedom to ignore what Jeneva suggested. He thought he might be able to figure things out if only he could act the part himself.

It was almost six o'clock. The people who had performances that evening were hurrying out. Through the open fire door the evening sunlight angled in, fragrant with sun-warmed earth and petunias. Lucas could hear people playing baseball at the diamond just down the hill from the theatre. Jeneva spoke briefly to Everett, who scribbled something in his red notebook, locked the fire door, and went out the hall door after her. Other people followed them: Alex, wiping his forehead with a towel and muttering to Meredith; Brian Able, who played Fleance's father Banquo; poker-faced Jon Crowell, who had waited all afternoon to say his first lines as the suspicious Macduff only to have the scene stopped and restarted every time before getting there; Norris and Adam, running lines as they went. At last only Lucas and the new First Witch, Dana Sloe, remained.

She had watched the rehearsal all day, though none of the witch scenes had been scheduled. When breaks were called she joined the chat around the coffee urn, but Lucas noticed that she smiled a lot more than she spoke. She was back from lunch as early as he was, wandering the length of the shelving along one of the walls and fingering the rehearsal props that had already accumulated there. He tried to read a book someone had left behind, but every now and then, without meaning to, his eyes sought out Dana Sloe. Once she caught him looking at her, and her own eyes stared back at him, shiny and expressionless over her chubby cheeks and disarmingly girlish smile.

Now she nodded at him in a friendly way from across the room. "You're Fleance," she said.

"Actually, I'm Lucas Cormier."

"And you want to be Macbeth," she said.

He was taken aback. Had his longing shown so clearly that a perfect stranger could read it in his face? "It's a great role," he said as coolly as he could. "Who wouldn't want to play it?" And then, without meaning to, he blurted out, "You called the Thane by his name."

She gave a tiny laugh, but no other answer. Lucas didn't want to be alone with her any longer. "Well, goodbye," he said, turning toward the hall door.

"I'm heading that way, too," she said pleasantly.

It would have been rude not to wait for her. As she joined him she said, "What do you think of Alexander Blair's Macbeth?"

Lucas wasn't superstitious, not even a little bit, but he wished Dana Sloe would stop using Macbeth's real name. "Alex is a good actor," he said evasively.

"He may be that," the woman said, "but he's not a good Macbeth."

Her eyes weren't shiny now, Lucas noticed. Their blue had paled, and there was a cloud of white around each iris that made them look old and weary. "I've been watching you," she said after a moment. "You seem to have an almost protective feeling about Macbeth. Are you Scottish?"

"American."

"Your heritage, I mean."

"I'm American," Lucas repeated stubbornly.

"The Scots revere Macbeth. He's been dead more than a thousand years, but they look on him as the last real Scottish monarch."

They were out in the corridor now, deserted except for the two of them. "Did you know Joan Mackenzie?" Lucas asked suddenly.

"Joan Mackenzie?"

"The actor you replaced."

"Ah. No, I didn't know her." She added politely, "I'm so bad at names. Take that young girl in the company. I met her this morning –"

"Christine Gale? The Third Witch, you mean?"

"No, not her. Another one." They were negotiating a narrow spot in the corridor between racks of half-finished costumes. "She brought me a cup of coffee."

"You mean Kinny," Lucas said. "But she's not an actor."

"Kinny? What an odd name."

"It's Kincardine, really. Kincardine O'Neil."

Dana stopped abruptly. One hand reached for a costume on the rack beside her. She stared at it for a long moment. "Lovely fabric," she said.

It was cloth of gold, expensive and beautiful. All the same, Lucas wasn't at all sure that it was the fabric that had brought Dana Sloe to that sudden halt. "I've forgotten my script," he said. "I'd better go back for it."

She moved her hand from the fabric to his forearm, stopping him. It was a light contact, her fingertips barely brushing his skin. But he was jolted by it; her fingers were cold and very dry and seemed to be feeling for something. He drew away hastily. Her eyelids drooped. It was the first time he had seen her anything but round-eyed. "Where is the Props Department?"

"To your right," he said, pointing to a door just down the corridor. "Wardrobe's first, then Soft Props — that's cushions, masks, anything made of cloth that's needed in the plays here."

"And the other props?"

"They're made in Carpentry. That's just beyond Soft Props. Why do you —?" He broke off.

She smiled. "Just trying to find my way around. I'll see you tomorrow."

When Lucas got back to the rehearsal hall, its emptiness startled him. He had never been in it all by himself before. The tape on the floor outlined the exact shape of the Festival stage upstairs. What would it be like to be on that stage, all by himself? He stepped out into the taped-off area, imagining himself at the bottom of a series of steps, rising to the stage. Behind him, around him, was a theatre, tier upon tier of seats. The house lights were off. He could hear the rustle of programmes, little coughs; and from the nearer seats, expensive perfumes wafted. The spotlight was on, waiting for him — for Macbeth, not Fleance. Lucas went to center stage, nodded dismissal to an imaginary servant, and said, *"Is this a dagger which I see before me, the handle toward my hand? Come, let me clutch thee —"*

The famous scene unrolled. Lucas knew all the lines by heart. He tried it Alexander Blair's way, but knew he hadn't got it right. He tried it Jeneva's way, making Macbeth simply and purely evil, and that didn't work either. The man was just not like that.

Lucas closed his eyes, imagining a bloody dagger hanging in the air in front of him. Deep in the castle Lady Macbeth was drugging King Duncan's servants and making everything ready for Macbeth to come in and murder the king. The bell would tell him when. There was no one to do it but him.

He had killed in war, but that was necessity. This was choice. Or was it?

Out on the heath were three witches who knew, absolutely knew, that Macbeth was going to be king. But Duncan had already named his son Malcolm as his preference for the kingship when he died. Malcolm was too young now to make an effective king. If Duncan died now, the thanes would be certain to go against his wishes and elect the more experienced Macbeth to the throne. But the longer Duncan lived, the older and more experienced Malcolm would get, and the more likely it would be that the thanes would endorse Duncan's choice. Which meant, if the witches were right and Macbeth was going to be king instead of Malcolm, that Duncan had to die now.

And the witches had to be right. They had known ahead of time that Macbeth would be named Thane of Cawdor, and so he had been. Why should they be wrong about the kingship?

Witches who knew. A bloody apparition of a dagger. Signs from hell. Logic.

Lucas opened his eyes. He began again. He was Macbeth, trapped by a logical mind, and by hell. *Is this a dagger which I see before me, the handle toward my hand?* The horror was right, now, the feeling of doom. He could do nothing but what had been planned for him. Everything was set out, even the terrible results of what he had to do. *Now o'er the one half-world nature seems dead.* He was going to murder Duncan and nature at the same time.

He was shaking when he finished. There was applause, but he hardly noticed. He had got Macbeth right. It was only one scene, and Macbeth would change as the play went on, but for this moment, he had got the man right.

"That was great, Lucas," said a soft voice.

With a great effort, Lucas shook off the role he'd been playing. Kinny was standing in the doorway, smiling at him shyly. Gruffly he said, "Dumb, eh? Playing to an empty house."

"I came down to see if the rehearsal was finished. I hope you don't mind that I watched."

"I thought you'd have gone home long ago."

She flushed slightly. "I was supposed to go shopping with Jean — she's in the Props Department too — but then Jim asked her to stay late to fix something that had broken in rehearsal, and so —"

He wasn't interested in any of this. He had got Shakespeare's Macbeth right, and he wanted to think about it. "I've got to go," he said.

She was still standing in the doorway. He brushed by her on his way out. She was looking down at the floor, but he knew he'd hurt her feelings. "Sorry," he said. It was all he could manage. He had to be by himself.

❋ ❋ ❋

THERE WAS A NEW BOARDER at Granny's Attic. Kinny found out about it at breakfast on Friday, the day after she had started working in the Props Department. Mrs. Palfrey was serving the electrician Andrew Vance his bacon and eggs and asking Kinny if she was sure she wouldn't have anything but toast, when the dining room door opened.

Eyes, Kinny thought. She was facing the window opposite the door. Slowly she turned her head, and saw Dana Sloe in the doorway.

Round blue eyes peered uncertainly into the

dining room, met Kinny's gaze, searched on, and stopped at Mrs. Palfrey. "I'm late, sorry," she said, with an apologetic smile. "Doesn't that bacon smell good?"

Ordinary eyes, ordinary smile, ordinary voice saying ordinary things. Kinny relaxed. No one was watching her. Probably no one ever had been watching her.

Mrs. Palfrey introduced the three of them, then went back to the kitchen. "We've met before," Dana said, smiling at Kinny.

"I got you a cup of coffee in the morning rehearsal," Kinny replied. She said nothing about the second time she had seen the other woman. On her way to the rehearsal hall last night she had noticed Dana standing against the end wall of Soft Props, surrounded by huge bolts of textiles and staring into the larger Carpentry Workshop across the way.

Kinny had been going to say hello, but Dana had seemed to be concentrating intently on some private thought of her own, and so she had just walked by.

"I think I saw you in the Props Department at the end of the day, too," Dana said, pouring cream into her coffee. "You were talking to another woman in there, something about shopping, I think."

"Yes," Kinny said. That had been quite a long time before she herself had seen Dana.

How long had the older woman been standing in Soft Props anyway?

"Here's your breakfast, Ms. Sloe," Mrs. Palfrey said, whisking into the dining room with a plate laden with eggs and bacon. "It's a bit the worse for wear, I'm afraid. I had it ready for the usual breakfast time." She emphasized the word 'usual'. "Help yourselves to more coffee." She was gone.

"I rather think I won't be late for breakfast from now on," Dana Sloe said wryly, poking at an egg with a fork and watching it bounce back.

"Mrs. Palfrey whips us all into shape first thing," Andrew said with a grin. "After that, she's fine. You were lucky to get in here. Mrs. P's usually booked solid."

Dana spread marmalade on a piece of toast. "Mmm. Homemade. The rooms are comfortable, I will say."

"You must have roasted last night, though," Andrew said. "When I came home at midnight it was still as hot as Hades out there, but you didn't even have your window open."

"*Do* they open?"

"Doesn't yours?" Kinny asked.

"All that ironwork in the way," Dana said vaguely. "Such a nuisance." She pushed her plate away. "I'm interested in your name, Kinny. Did you know there is a village called

Kincardine O'Neil in Scotland?"

Kinny nodded. "Most people have never heard of it."

"Have you ever visited there?"

"No. My Dad has, though. He's in the oil business, and was spending a lot of time in Scotland the year I was born. Mom was at home in Montreal. She doesn't like traveling. It turned out Dad was having lunch in Kincardine O'Neil at just about the exact minute I was born. Mom thought it'd be neat, seeing as my last name was O'Neil anyway, to name me after the town. Have you ever been there, Ms. Sloe?"

"Do call me Dana. Yes, I've been there. It's a very old village. A lot of interesting things have happened near it."

The bright light from the window seemed to have drained Dana's eyes of colour, turning them glittery and hard, like glass. But not ordinary glass, Kinny thought, not glass that you could see through. She thought of the one-way glass they had in department stores, glass that looked like mirrors so that people fixed their hair in front of them or checked to see if something was in their teeth. And all the time, invisible on the other side, there was somebody there, watching them.

"Dana's a pretty unusual name, too," Andrew said. "It's mostly given to men, isn't it?"

"Nowadays, I suppose," Dana said, rather coldly.

Andrew tossed back his coffee. "I've got a technical call in ten minutes. Does anybody want a ride over to the theatre?"

Kinny jumped eagerly to her feet. "Oh, yes, please. Jim asked me to come early today."

When she arrived, Jim met her at the door. "We didn't wear you out yesterday, then, lovie? Good stuff!" He winked. "I suppose, since it is Jeneva paying your salary, it would be only fair for you to check to see if she needs you for anything." She turned swiftly to go, but he called her back. "Not yet, lovie. Rehearsal's not till ten. You can wire a lot of leaves in an hour."

Later, Kinny excused herself and went to the rehearsal hall. Jeneva was in the center of a large group of people, all trying to get her attention. Kinny waited patiently. She saw Lucas come in, but he didn't look her way, and she was glad. His snub yesterday still rankled.

At last Jeneva was free, looking down at a script and frowning. Kinny cleared her throat. "Excuse me, Jeneva."

The director looked up. Her face closed. "Yes?"

Proudly, Kinny said, "Props wanted to know if I could work for them for the next week. Since you don't have anything for me to do, I thought –"

"What a good idea," Jeneva said. "You can

be making yourself useful and getting to know your way around this maze of a theatre at the same time." She smiled warmly, taking Kinny by surprise. "I'm impressed with your initiative, my dear. You'll be a pro here in no time." She gave Kinny a conspiratorial wink. "Your mother won't be quite as pleased about that as we are, though, will she?"

Kinny blushed. "She told you why she —?"

"It's all right, sweetheart. I've never been asked to be a bad example before, but I've known your mother a long time." She laughed, and it was such an infectious sound that Kinny couldn't help joining in.

"It's not you," Kinny said at last. "It's the theatre in general she wants me not to like."

"And now that you're here, what's the verdict? No, don't answer, the last few days have been too awful for anybody to judge fairly. You'll have to give us a chance to be normal for a while. But tell me, as someone from Quebec, what do you think of the setting for our play?"

Kinny swallowed. "I, well, I'm not...." Jeneva looked at her thoughtfully, and Kinny took a deep breath. "I wouldn't like it if I thought it was just an anti-French thing."

Jeneva's eyebrows angled downward. "Why, Kinny, what a very odd thing to say! There are so many reasons to set a play in an unusual historical context. Look at this one. In the last scene the English have won Scotland for Malcolm, who is as English as any born Englishman. But the fascinating thing is that when Shakespeare actually wrote the play, some five centuries after Malcolm took over, James I was King of England, and he was a Scot, the very first ever to rule England. So Scotland lost its own country to come back in Shakespeare's time to win it back – and rule England as well! Compare that to Canada. The English won Quebec in 1759, and now, more than two centuries later, the French have taken it back again. Not only that, they seem to have as much political power over the rest of Canada as James I had over England. That's just one of the ironies I'm interested in showing –"

"Ready for the Porter Scene, Jeneva," Everett Lunn called.

"Sorry darling, have to run," Jeneva said. "We'll chat another time, okay?"

It all sounded very plausible, Kinny had to admit. Maybe Adam and the others were being unfair to Jeneva, saying she was just out to get the Quèbècois. Obviously she had done a lot of research that the rest of them knew nothing about. All the same...Kinny tried to feel again the excitement and pride that had filled her when she'd first heard she would be working for Jeneva. But the most she could achieve was a hard-won and dubious open mind.

IT WAS FRIDAY, but nobody seemed to wind down for the weekend in the theatre. "I haven't forgotten about going shopping," Jean told Kinny at lunch that day, "but I have to meet somebody after work tonight, and tomorrow Jim's got me scheduled for a working lunch."

"What about the mirror? How's it going?"

"I started on it again this morning. First I couldn't find it, and I don't care what Tony says, it wasn't me who left it on his bench. Anyway, when I finally found it somebody had piled magazines on it and the paint stuck. I was so mad I could have eaten the damn thing."

"Do you want to look in some antique stores this weekend? I'll bet they'll be open on Sunday."

"I have to go to Hamilton to see my parents."

"Monday, then? We're off on Monday, aren't we?"

"I'm not coming back till Monday night." She shrugged apologetically.

"I could go by myself."

Jean hesitated. "You wouldn't know what to look for."

"You could draw me a picture."

"But you haven't got a car. The stores are all over town. How would you get around?"

Kinny sighed. "Jean, don't worry about it. If you don't want me to do it, I won't."

"I do want you to do it. It's just —" She bit her lip. "Hey, I've got a bike you could borrow."

"Sold," Kinny said, grinning. After a minute, Jean smiled, too.

Kinny went to see *The Miracle Worker* at the Avon that night. She liked the story about how a blind, mute, enraged child named Helen Keller was taught to function by a woman who had been blind herself. But she didn't at all like the way the teacher was played. Like somebody on a great big power trip, Kinny told herself in disgust. Doing all those amazing things to help Helen because it made her feel good about herself, not because she cared about Helen at all.

Granny's Attic was dark when Kinny got home. Only the light over the stairs was on as Kinny climbed the two flights to the floor where Mrs. Palfrey lodged her boarders. There were no lights on in the upstairs hall. Kinny looked for a switch, couldn't find it, and gave up. The staircase light cast a deformed shadow in front of her as she walked down the narrow corridor. None of the rooms showed any light under the door. She passed Andrew's room, silent. Then the bathroom, door ajar, one dripping faucet plunking regularly into the basin. Then Kinny's own room. Beyond that was Dana Sloe's, lost in shadows at the end of the hall.

The staircase light didn't reach this far. It was too dark to identify the contents of her purse. Kinny tried to find her bedroom key by feel. It eluded her. As she stood there scrabbling in her purse, she became aware that she was hearing something besides the regular drip of water.

Whispering, she thought. She stopped fumbling in her purse and stood very still. Someone was whispering in Dana Sloe's pitch black room at the end of the hall.

The hairs rose on Kinny's neck. Ordinary people didn't sit in the dark to talk. And why were they whispering? What were they afraid people would hear, if they spoke aloud?

She licked her lips. She remembered how Dana had stood for so long in Soft Props last night, watching her and Jean. She remembered the way Dana's eyes had gone all colourless and hard at breakfast this morning. They were different from those eyes that had looked at her in the darkness after Joan Mackenzie was killed — rounder, less ruthless, expressionless instead of desperate. But somehow, at this minute, they reminded her of them.

Slowly, quietly, she tiptoed closer to Dana's room.

"...too much iron. Drains me...not enough power left as it is."

Was she hearing it, or imagining it?

"...noticed it too." A louder whisper then, harsher. "The day the woman died I used a masking, and still that boy saw me! If a simple masking is unreliable..."

"...waste of power. Just watch him. And when we find it..."

"It is near. I feel it."

Kinny could feel herself trembling. She reached out a hand to the wall of the corridor, trying to steady herself. The whispering had stopped. With a sudden perfect clarity Kinny knew that the whisperers were listening for something. Her heart thudded. She skittered down the hall into the bathroom. With the door locked and the light on, she flushed the toilet, ran the water in the sink, and got her key out. Her hands were shaking. It took all her courage to open the bathroom door again.

But there was no movement in the dark hall, and no noise, not even a whisper.

CHAPTER SEVEN

LUCAS HATED MONDAYS IN STRATFORD. There were no rehearsals and no performances, and everybody who had anything interesting to do outside the town did it. Some Mondays there were parties, but not today. Joan Mackenzie's memorial service on Saturday had left people unsociable.

Lucas had gone to the service, sitting between Norris and Adam. The more he thought about it, the more unlikely it seemed that the live end of a ceiling wire could have been deliberately disconnected in front of all those people. Even if someone could have done it without being observed, how could that person get up there without a ladder? An acrobat might have managed, but not an elderly, humpbacked woman. Especially when that woman was somebody only he was sure had been there.

He had tried to banish the memory of that woman with her startled eyes glaring at him, but it kept coming back to him. He was thinking about her now, pacing his tiny room in the cheapest bed-and-breakfast in Stratford. He picked up a magazine, dropped it again. He sat down on his bed and looked at the mirror across from him. His reflection looked oddly unfamiliar to his own eyes. Older somehow. Dispossessed.

He couldn't sit still. There was something he should do. He knew it, but he didn't know what it was. He got to his feet and began pacing again. It was very hot in his room. Sweat made triangles in his shirt. Outside his window, which opened only a crack, a sere wind buffeted the trees. Strips of beige paint on the window-sill stood up like curling ribbon. Over the hoots and applause from a TV game show downstairs Lucas could hear the distant whistle of a train. It was a lonely sound, a going-away sound. He thought of Chicago, and Cohoes, New York; he thought of Scotland, where Macbeth had been born.

Funny how until coming to Stratford, he had never considered the fact that Macbeth had been a real man from a real place, and not just a character Shakespeare had invented. What had he been like as a person? He decided to go to the library to find out.

The sun beat down on him as he walked up Downie Street. Kids licked ice cream and jumped curbs on their skateboards. Tourists stood in front of the Avon Theatre, taking pictures of each other reading the playbill. A street artist, bald head dripping sweat, squatted on the sidewalk, painting. Flower-boxes rippled with purple and pink and the sharp smell of geraniums. Turning left and heading toward the library, Lucas saw a haze over the river to the north. He thought he could smell that, too.

In the small, pleasant-looking library he found exactly what he was looking for. It was a short book, non-fiction; he read it on the spot.

Duncan was a vicious tyrant...not only heartless but totally incapable of basic military strategy.

So much for Shakespeare's wonderful old King Duncan! He hadn't been old, and he hadn't been good. He had ruled only five years when he died, and he died on the battlefield, not while sleeping in Macbeth's house. Not only had Macbeth not murdered Duncan in the treacherous way Shakespeare had described, it wasn't even certain that Macbeth had been the one to inflict the battle wounds that killed his king. And after Duncan's death, Macbeth got the kingship through an ordinary election, not, as Shakespeare said, by unlawfully taking it.

Macbeth was a liberal king, fair and tall. A Saint Berchan, who lived at the time, said of him, *Very pleasant was that handsome youth to me. Brimful of food was Scotland, east and west, during the reign of the brave, ruddy king.*

Then, in 1054, young Malcolm Canmore, son of the dead King Duncan, claimed that he had more right to the Scottish kingship than did Macbeth, who had now ruled for almost 15 years. Blood-inheritance of the monarchy was not recognized by Scottish law. But Malcolm had grown up in the court of the English King Edward, who believed in the right of a son to ascend the throne after his father. Also, Edward did not like having strong King Macbeth on his northern borders. To help the weaker Malcolm in his bid for the kingship, Edward sent an army to attack Macbeth at Dunsinane. Macbeth was defeated, but not killed there, though that was what Shakespeare had said. Macbeth fled to the north, rallied, and fled again. After three years he was killed by Malcolm near a stone circle just outside the village of Lumphanan to the north of the River Dee. Malcolm had cut off Macbeth's head. In the play Shakespeare had made Macduff responsible for the decaptitation, not Malcolm, but at least he'd got the cause of death right.

Thoughtfully, Lucas closed the book. Then he opened it again, leafing back through it. There was a lot of stuff about the peace and prosperity in Scotland during Macbeth's reign, his legal reforms, his support for orphans and women, his gifts to the Celtic Church. Nowhere could Lucas find any reference to a grim reign of terror, or to the bloody and tyrannical Macbeth of Shakespeare's play. The bloody and tyrannical king had been Duncan, not Macbeth. As history, Shakespeare's *Macbeth* was apparently not much more than a pack of lies.

Maybe it wouldn't have made such a good play to have told the truth. Certainly it was politically safer not to make King Duncan the villain, with Shakespeare's own king, James, related to Duncan, supposedly through Banquo's line. There were probably artistic reasons for switching Macbeth's and Duncan's characters as well. But now, because of Shakespeare, most people in the world thought that Macbeth had been evil, when in fact he'd been an honourable man and a good king.

It was a sobering thought. Lucas left the library, still feeling very restless. Crossing Church Street, he saw Kinny riding a bicycle up from the bridge toward him. The wind had loosened her ponytail, and long honey-coloured curls bounced around her face. Her cheeks were pink with exertion and heat. She was looking straight ahead. Obviously she hadn't seen him. Or maybe she had, and was remembering how he'd snubbed her the other night, when she'd watched him play Macbeth in the empty rehearsal hall. Maybe she was expecting him to snub her again.

"Hey, Kinny!" he called.

Her head jerked up. Her face looked uncertain. Then she pedaled over to him. She put one foot to the ground and one hand to her hair, an instinctive movement toward the rubber band dangling from a single long curl.

"Don't," he said, surprising himself.

"Don't what?"

"Don't tie up your hair. It looks nice out of the pony tail. When you pull it back too hard —" He broke off, put four fingers on either side of his own face, and pushed toward his ears. "All bone, see?"

"When you're an actor it's good to have bones," Kinny said. She grabbed her rebellious hair with one hand and wrapped the rubber band tightly around it with the other. Her cheekbones jutted. "There," she said defiantly.

Obviously she *was* mad at him. "You being a tourist today?" he asked, nodding at a Tourist Information bag hanging from her handlebars.

"No, I'm looking for a mirror," she said. She got even pinker. "Not for me," she added quickly, "for Props. For Jean, actually. She's been trying to make one for the Apparitions Scene, but the glass keeps going weird, so I said we should try antique stores, but she couldn't come with me, so I —" She broke off.

"Where have you tried?"

"All over. Five places. No, six. The tourist bureau gave me a list. There are only a couple of stores left. They're on York Street."

"You've passed York. It's back where you crossed the bridge."

"Oh."

"Want some company?" He didn't know why

he offered. He didn't even like shopping.

"You haven't got a bike."

"It's only a block away," he said. "If you wanted, you could push your bike that far. Or I could."

She pursed her lips. "Okay," she said at last.

Not exactly enthusiastic, he thought. Well, he deserved it. Snubbing her last week, and now, criticizing her hair. Where was the famous Lucas Cormier kindness to little girls?

"I'll treat you to an ice cream cone afterward," he said, taking the handlebars from her in a gentlemanly way.

"I never eat ice cream," she replied coldly.

It was Monday, and there wasn't anything else to do. "So you'll watch me eat one," he said.

THE FIRST ANTIQUE STORE contained more furniture than smaller items, and had that dauntingly well-arranged look that meant high price tags. The clerk looked up from her catalog when Kinny told her what she was looking for and how much Jean thought they'd be able to pay. "Maybe you should try flea markets," she said disdainfully.

The second store was much the same. "Well, that's that," Kinny said dispiritedly, as they came out. "There aren't any more stores on the list." She showed it to him.

"Did you look in the phone book to see if there are any others in the Yellow Pages?"

"No, but —"

He turned back to the store. "What are you doing?" she called after him.

"I'm going to borrow their phone book."

"Listen, Lucas, it doesn't matter. It was just an idea Jean and I had. It doesn't —" The door swung shut behind him.

She sighed in exasperation. She was hot and tired, and her knees hurt from banging them into the handlebars of Jean's bike. All she wanted was to go back to Grannie's Attic and have a cool shower. She wondered why Lucas was suddenly so keen on this wild goose chase. Or did he just think she was, and was trying to show her he was sorry for snapping at her the other day?

Grumpily she squatted to unlock Jean's bicycle chain. Without warning she became aware that someone was watching her. Her chin jerked up, the padlock dropping from her hand. Like a dog sniffing for a scent she turned her head one way, then another. She knew what she was looking for — eyes that were desperate and icy and ruthless, eyes that had been searching for something for a long time.

What did they *want* from her? Why did they keep haunting her like this?

Quickly she stood up, staring down the short street. A busload of elderly people was crossing the road to get to the gardens by the river. None of them paid the least attention to anything on Kinny's side of the street. A woman was coming out of the indoor mall a few steps away. She looked casually at Kinny, but her eyes weren't at all like the ones Kinny was worried about. An old married couple strolled hand-in-hand nearby. Not them. Three teenagers with a ghetto-blaster. An athletic-looking man on a bicycle. It was no good. There was no one watching her. She was just being paranoid.

"You okay?" Lucas asked, at her elbow. "You look upset."

The eyes weren't there. She was imagining them. They weren't there! She took a deep breath. "Did you find anything?"

"One. Sort of. It calls itself a second-hand shop. But antiques are mostly second-hand, so I thought —"

She was hardly listening. Even if the eyes were there, they didn't have to affect her like this. Like Friday night, when she'd locked herself in her room and turned on both lights and sat shivering in bed because of a little bit of whispering down the hall. After an hour she had figured it out. Dana Sloe hadn't been sitting there in the dark whispering to someone. She'd been muttering in her sleep, that was all. People did that all the time. There was nothing sinister about it.

"It's called Times Past," Lucas was saying. "You want to go there?"

"What?"

"To the second-hand store," Lucas said patiently.

Kinny was straining her eyes across the road toward the river. There was someone standing alone there on the riverbank. A woman, facing away from the river. She was old, and there was something strange about her shape. Twisted, maybe? Or hunched? She was too far away for Kinny to be sure.

"It's just off St. David Street," Lucas said. "We may as well check it out."

A rusty old delivery van rumbled to a halt in front of them. As if a shutter had fallen, the feeling of being watched went away. Kinny nodded abruptly. "Okay," she said to Lucas. She bent to finish unlocking Jean's bicycle.

"Why not come back for the bike later?" Lucas suggested. "No fun pushing that thing all the way to St. David. And it'll save us a couple of blocks if we cut through the mall here."

The van would pull away, and the bike would still be here. That woman on the riverbank might think they were in one of the stores. She might wait for quite a while to be sure. By the time she guessed what had happened, they'd be long gone.

Kinny nodded quickly. "Let's go."

She didn't care about that store. She didn't

hold out much hope for finding a mirror there for Jean. All she wanted was to get away from those eyes.

※ ※ ※

TIMES PAST WAS A CONVERTED GARAGE, a small, grim building behind someone's house. It had two iron-barred windows unsuccessfully tarted up with red and white gingham curtains and a prison-like steel door under a fancy gothic sign. There was a false window painted on the door, curtained with equally fake gingham. The wider metal door that had once allowed entrance for cars was padlocked to hooks on either side and had been painted in checkerboard squares to match the gingham, red and white. The effect was blindingly awful.

Kinny shook her head doubtfully. "You really want to go in there?"

"We've come this far," Lucas said.

They went in. It was startlingly cool and dim after the glare and the heat outside. As they hesitated in the doorway, letting their eyes get accustomed to the lower light, the door swung shut behind them.

"May I help you?" a man's voice said, as if he was sure he couldn't.

"I'm looking for a hand mirror," Kinny said. "Not too expensive."

The man came forward. He had cocker

spaniel eyes and looked like someone who had tried and tried and lost every time. "I think I've got one," he said hopefully. "If it's still here, it's with the pile of stuff I got in last week. I've been too busy to sort it. Tourist season. I'm hardly able to keep my head above water."

Lucas was impatient with the obvious lie. Kinny saw how he kept shifting from one foot to the other, his eyes darting around the shop, his fingers flexing against his thighs.

"It was a job lot," the man went on. "Collection of theatre props, actually. The old fellow who'd owned it had travelled all over, picking up this and that in theatre towns all over England. His son got all his stuff when he died, and I bought what he didn't have room for. Some interesting things." He smiled doubtfully.

The shop was as dirty as a litterbox. The man's spaniel eyes seemed to be expecting them to go away. Kinny looked at his skinny wrists poking out of those too-short sleeves. She cleared her throat, and said, "Where might the mirror be?"

"Back of the store," the man said, "on the end counter. You might have to move a few things. Or I could –"

"We'll manage," Lucas said.

He didn't wait for Kinny, striding ahead down the narrow aisle in the center of the store. When she got to the back he was already sorting

through one end of a heap of disreputable looking objects. She began at the other. Three ceram-
ic masks, a bowl full of grimy waxed fruit all
glued together, a frilly parasol, a piggy bank –
already her fingers felt filthy. A teatowel, with "A
Present From Brighton" embroidered on it and
a handwritten tag pinned near the hem. She
made out the words, "from the first Welsh performance of –" and then something about N.
Coward.

"Depressing, isn't it?" Lucas said.

Near the bottom of the pile was a heap of
soiled lace antimacassars. She dug into them to
see if that was all there was. Her fingertips
brushed against something hard. She took a
quick look at Lucas. He was burrowing through
some old clothing, paying no attention to her.
Quietly, almost furtively, she lifted the antimacassars away.

The mirror was lying face down, so that at
first glance it looked to be made entirely of
wood. The wood was dark, almost black, though
it hadn't been painted. There were no visible
seams, and hardly any grain. It looked as if it had
been carved from a single piece of wood. There
were no decorative details, but the carving was
expert, and very smooth. There was one ugly,
shallow gouge in the handle. It was the only flaw
that Kinny could discern, but it was very noticeable because it was a different colour than the

rest of the wood, a deep reddish-brown. Like a burn, Kinny thought, or old dried blood. She looked at it for a long while without touching it. Jean could fix it, or disguise it, if the other side was in good enough condition to make the effort worthwhile.

She should look at the other side.

Her heart was pounding. Her hands gripped the edge of the counter. Look at the other side of the mirror, idiot. It's what you're here for. Look.

"Kinny?"

Lucas's voice. He'd noticed she'd found something. She made her right hand let go of the counter. She forced it to reach for the handle of the mirror. Her hand and her arm, the counter and the mirror – two small, slow universes reaching out to each other. And then Lucas's impatient hand flicked under hers, picked up the mirror, turned it, and pressed the scarred handle into her palm. His hand remained on hers, the handle of the mirror between them. The glass was a strange, shiny blue. Their two faces rippled in it, staring at each other with unfamiliar eyes.

Lucas's withdrew, slowly, almost reluctantly. Now Kinny was alone in the glass; only she was not alone, there was someone else there, a shadow of a face, ancient beyond understanding. The glass blurred. Kinny leaned closer. Moonlight and grey stones, closer and closer, smoke in the distance, moaning. Closer still — liver-spotted hands, cracked as a desert, one holding a mirror, the other arranging white flowers in blue-black hair. Old, oh so old....

My hands were fair once, fair as this girl's. Now they disgust me. I would be rid of this aged body!

My sisters know my impatience; they nod to each other, and to me. "Soon," that nod says, "soon." The girl with her greedy little mouth is preparing herself. An hour or two, no more, and it will be done. But the girl is not as calm as she must be; the songs of Malcolm's men are distant, but they worry her.

"This is a Goddess Ring," I remind her. "The wars of men come not here."

"They say the king's forces are sore pressed." Still frightened, plucking a blossom from her blue-black hair, tearing at it. "What if the king comes here for help, and his enemies follow?"

"Speak to her, Sister," I say impatiently. "I have lost my skill at Mothering the young."

My middle sister smiles her wide toothy smile, puts an arm around the girl, kisses her perfunctorily. "Armies do not move at night," she says.

The girl shifts uneasily, looks unconvinced. My sister is not as good at this as she used to be. It is boredom, of course. She wants to get on. In every way she is growing into me, whom men call Hag. But until the ceremony is over, she must remain Mother. My youngest sister stirs anxiously. It is she who yearns to comfort that frightened girl, but she is

Maiden, old though she is, unfulfilled and childless. She must turn Mother soon, or she will wither and grow bitter and cold. I know. I have been what they are now. I will be them again.

"When this night is over," I tell the girl, "you shall be one of us, and need fear no army anywhere."

"I will not die? Ever?"

"All bodies die," my youngest sister answers. "Yours will, too. But it will live long and age slowly; it will be young and beautiful when your grandchildren's grandchildren are old."

The girl smiles, triangular and sleek. "And men will still admire me?"

"Even more than they do now."

I have had enough of this. It is always the same, after all. "The moon is rising," I say. "We must get on."

The girl hears the boredom in my voice. She grows hostile. "What about you?" she says to me. "When the Spell is done I will be Maiden, and the other Maiden will become the Mother. And the Mother will be —"

"She will be me. She will be Hag."

"And what will happen to you?"

"There are only three Sisters. Your body will contain one of them. It is what the ceremony achieves. A blending, more or less."

She hears the words. They always hear the words, and they never absorb them. "I will have power," she says. "You said it. I will have your power."

"You will be Maiden. You will have my power." I say it wearily. It is what she wants. It is what they all want. It *is why she is here. She has chosen it.*

"Sister! The king comes!"

He strides alone into the Goddess Ring, iron-garbed and weaponed, thinking nothing of his arrogance. It is the way of men, finally to request what they have always spurned, and be angry when it is no longer there for them. I say what I must. He leaves. We begin our ceremony.

The weaving. The wraithing. The awakening and the opening. I am inside the looking glass, where I must be for what remains to be done. Inside the glass I can look out, I can hear. I see when he comes back. I see what he does. But I am here, I cannot stop it, it is too late. An explosion of light, white, then blue, and screaming, screaming, and the glass blurring, I cannot see, Goddess help me, I cannot....

"...all right? Kinny? Kinny!"

"I can't see!"

"Why not? Kinny?"

She dragged her eyes from the mirror. There was a man staring at her. A beard, a sword, iron in a Goddess Ring. How dare he?

Hands on her shoulders, shaking her. "Kinny!"

She blinked. No beard. No sword. It was Lucas. He looked as if he'd seen a ghost.

"What's the matter?" she got out.

"What do you mean, What's the matter? You just about passed out...."

She got hold of herself, threw back her head, took a deep breath. "I never pass out," she said.

"I was just feeling a bit...tired. The heat. And all that bike riding. I'm fine, Lucas, really."

He stared at her doubtfully. Then he shook his head. "Sure. Okay. But the way you were staring into that mirror...." He made as if to take it from her, but she hugged it to her chest. He shrugged. "You going to buy it for Jean?"

"For —?" She paused. "Yes. Yes, I'm going to buy it."

"Maybe you'd better find out what it costs, first."

"It'll be the right price." She was sure it would be. It would have to be.

"You're not going to spend your own money on it, are you? Don't you think you should check with Jean first?"

"It'll be all right."

Blindly she turned away from him, holding the mirror tightly, not letting herself look into it again. It was hard to hand it over to the man at the counter. He talked the whole time he was wrapping it. "Good shape..." she heard. "...sandpaper'll do fine...genuine...." And then, a whole sentence. "You could resilver the glass."

Kinny's voice was very clear when she replied. "I won't be doing that." She took the paper bundle the man handed her, and left.

Chapter Eight

ALL AFTERNOON KINNY THOUGHT ABOUT THE mirror — walking along the river trying to eat ice cream with Lucas walking silent and aloof at her side; checking the riverbank for the woman with the watching eyes; riding home on Jean's bike with the mirror in its bundle of tissue paper making a bump in the Tourist Information bag. What on earth had happened to her in that second-hand shop? If she'd been a daydreamer, she might have understood it. But she wasn't. She'd never in her life seen anything in a mirror except what ought to be there.

Until today.

That moonlit stone ring, like a smaller Stonehenge; the people in it, so fully formed, so real. The dark-haired girl with her greedy eyes and her mouth like a cat. The man with his sword and his desperation, facing down those three women: the Mother with her toothy kisses, the apple-cheeked Maiden, the Hag. In her dream — or whatever it had been — Kinny had known the Hag's thoughts, and they horrified her. Jaded, intolerant, so totally without illusions....

Sitting cross-legged on her bed with a hot

night breeze blowing on her face and the bundled mirror unopened on her lap, Kinny tried to consider it detachedly. It had all seemed so real. But how could it have been? A magical ceremony that made an old woman vanish into thin air and materialize inside the glass of a mirror; then something awful happening that kept that woman trapped in the mirror for centuries until somebody came along and bought the mirror from a second-hand shop? Kinny shook her head. It didn't make sense. It was stupid to imagine that it did.

But if there really was an old, old woman imprisoned in this mirror in her lap, confined in a single-dimensional cage with only her memories to keep her company, ages and ages of loneliness, of hating the man who had put her there....

It made Kinny shudder.

There was a knock on her door, soft, furtive. "Kinny? Are you awake? Kinny?"

Kinny's head jerked around, alarmed. Dana Sloe's voice. What did she want? It was almost midnight. It had been almost midnight when Kinny had heard those whispers in Dana's room the other night. She didn't want to see Dana Sloe right now. Maybe she could pretend to be asleep. But no, her light would be showing under the hall door. "Just a minute," she called.

She started for the door, leaving the parcel on

the bed. Somehow that worried her. She stopped, then got the parcel and placed it inside the fireplace, locking the cast-iron screen in front.

"Dumb, dumb, dumb," she muttered to herself. She pasted on a smile and opened her door. "Hi, Dana," she said.

"Hi, yourself." Her apple cheeks were innocent, her lips smiling. She was wearing a bathrobe, a depressingly youthful style, all flowers and frills. With her fair hair tumbling over her shoulders and her round, perpetually surprised, naked eyes, she looked disarmingly like someone whose photo might turn up in a magazine under the heading "Wanted: Beauty Makeover."

"I saw your light," Dana said. "Hope you don't mind me knocking so late. I keep forgetting to give you this at breakfast."

She held out a thin blue pamphlet. On the cover was printed in large letters, "In and Around: Grampian Highlands." Below it, even larger, were the words "KINCARDINE O'NEIL."

Wonderingly, Kinny took the pamphlet. It was only a single sheet folded in three. There was a sketch of what looked like an old, roofless church on the front; on the back, a large-scale map. Inside the foldout was a short history of the village of Kincardine O'Neil in Scotland, with tourist information about nearby places of interest.

Dana moved a little distance into the door-way, checked herself, and smiled apologetically. It seemed the most natural thing in the world to step back and let her in. "Would you like to sit down?" Kinny asked, uneasily indicating the only chair in the room. It was in front of the fireplace.

"No, thanks. I've been sitting all night." She wandered over to the chest of drawers and peered at herself in the mirror that hung over it. "I've been meaning to give you that pamphlet ever since I found out your name. Odd coincidence that I'd have it with me and meet the village's namesake in Stratford."

"It is odd," Kinny said.

"I have quite a lot of Scottish stuff with me, actually. My friend – the one I was staying with in Toronto – is planning a trip to Scotland, and asked me to bring her some tourist pamphlets. She's decided against the Grampians, so you can keep that one."

"Thanks," Kinny said. Suddenly she felt ashamed. How cold she was being to someone who had only ever been nice to her! "I feel really connected to that village," she said with an anxious smile, "even though I've never been there."

"Names do make connections. Especially the old names." Dana's voice sounded tired. "It has repercussions, giving an old name to a person."

"What do you mean?"

"A true name is more than a label. From oldest times a true name has been a kind of summing up of all the important attributes of a thing, or a person."

Kinny stared at her. "I don't –"

All of a sudden Dana laughed. Her face went very young and likeable. "Of course you don't! I'm talking in riddles. I guess all I'm saying is that names can have power."

Kinny said, "Like in the olden days, when sorcerers hid their real names so that other sorcerers couldn't have power over them?"

"That's right. And everybody knows somebody who has named a child after a certain lucky individual hoping that the luck would rub off."

"What if you're named for a place, like me?"

Dana's voice grew somehow more careful. "I suppose it would depend on whether the place had been lucky or unlucky, and whom it had been lucky or unlucky for." She seemed deeply interested in a bit of rough skin on her thumb. "If some very powerful event happened near a place long ago and you gave the name of that place to a modern child, that might link the child to the ancient event, or to its power. The right kind of child, I mean. Someone...sympathetic." She gazed at Kinny then, but her round eyes were completely expressionless.

Something was being said here, something Kinny didn't understand. She didn't like the way Dana was looking at her. She lifted her chin. "We've talked a lot about my name. What about yours? Does it have...power?"

Dana drew herself upright. There was no longer anything likeable in her face. She looked dried up and tired and astonishingly formidable. "Danu was the name of the original Goddess," she said, "the first religion of peoples everywhere in the world. She was the Goddess of the Earth, and the Moon, and of giving birth and being born. And in between, she grew old, and then she was the Goddess of Death. Dana is a variant of her original name. And Sloe is the fruit of her magical blackthorn tree. Together they make a name not to be taken lightly."

"Did your parents know all that, when they named you?" Kinny asked, hoping she sounded more normal than she felt. "Or is it a stage name?" But who would name herself after a goddess, even to be theatrical?

Dana was silent for a moment. Then she shrugged. "Must it be one thing or the other?" Steadily and without fuss she made her way to the door. She stopped there, then turned to face Kinny. "There are other old things besides names that retain their ancient power in these modern times. If you should ever find such a thing and be tempted to use it, do not keep it to yourself, Kincardine O'Neil. Let those who know more teach you how."

The door closed behind her. Kinny's heart was pounding. "If you should ever find such a thing...." Did Dana know about the mirror? But how could she? "Don't keep it to yourself." Keep it to herself! She had no intention in the world of keeping it, or using it, whatever that meant. She would give it to Jean in the morning, and Props could do what they wanted with it, and that would be the end of it as far as Kinny was concerned. Dana Sloe with her self-invented stage name would see that Kinny had no intention of getting involved with her, or with any of her melodramatic talk of old *repercussions.*

She almost ran to the fireplace. She unlocked the screen and jerked it aside. The tissue-wrapped bundle lay there, sootily anonymous. She would put it in her backpack right away, where she wouldn't have to see it. She got a hand on it and pulled; it snagged on a rough edge of the grate. Impatiently, she pulled again. She heard the paper tear. Gritting her teeth, she dug her hand under it, lifting from beneath. The paper was still intact, more or less. She scrambled to her feet. Where was her backpack? There, by the chair.

She didn't mean it to happen. She had meant never to look in the mirror again. But when she put the bundle on the seat of the chair, the paper somehow fell away, revealing the shiny blue glass of the mirror. She was bending over the chair already; her eyes were caught; she couldn't look away.

A serious, determined face, very young, peered at her out of a curtain of honey-coloured hair woven with white blossoms. She looked fey, lush as wild raspberries and inno-cent as a fawn. Her eyes were huge and green, and the smooth skin over her high cheekbones glowed. Dark brows, wide, soft mouth...Kinny blinked with shock. She was looking at herself. But she looked so strange, almost beautiful. And those flowers! The same as that dark-haired catty girl had worn. She reached up, slowly, to touch her hair, and felt it drawn tightly back into its usual ponytail, undecorat-ed with flowers or anything else.

You will be Maiden. You will have my power.

Familiar words, a familiar ancient voice. The Hag had said this to the other girl. Now she was saying it to Kinny.

"Not me. I'm not like that girl. I don't want power." Kinny said it. She knew she said it. But the lips of the girl in the mirror didn't move.

What do you want, then? What do you wish for?

What did she wish for? Kinny's lips twisted. To stop seeing things in this mirror, first of all! To be allowed to work for Jeneva. To be so good at what she did that everybody would know it wasn't just because of her parents' pull that she was here. To have people like Lucas and Adam and the others stop treating her like a kid and take her seriously, for a change.

"I don't want anything," Kinny said.

Into the mirror came fog, as if she had breathed against a frosty window. Her own fey, beautiful image grew fuzzier and fuzzier and finally disappeared altogether. There was nothing solid in the mirror now, only mist. Then that, too, disappeared, and her own white, scared, *real* face returned. Skinned-back hair tight to her head, forehead naked and enormous, eyes narrowed by the pull of her hair, cheeks like axe-blades over cavernous hollows beneath. No wonder Lucas liked her hair better down! She tore at the elastic of her ponytail, and her hair tumbled around her face.

That was better. She licked her lips and wiped the sweat off her forehead with the sleeve of her shirt, then with a deliberate movement raised her eyes from the mirror, got her backpack open and stuffed the mirror into it. She stepped back from the chair. Her stomach bubbled like a cauldron.

"I'm hearing things and I'm seeing things and I think I'm going out of my mind," she said aloud.

Dana's pamphlet was on the bed. Kinny crumpled it in a ball and made as if to throw it away. Then she stopped herself. Dana had given it to her for a reason. She had better find out why.

She smoothed it out and began to read. It seemed to be a perfectly innocent tourist pamphlet. Kincardine O'Neil was on the site of the ancient ford over the River Dee, and was at the crossroads of the two oldest roads in Scotland. From earliest times it had been a rest stop for cattle drovers on their journeys north and south. The church had been built in 1233. Nowadays, golf and fishing were the biggest activities. Places of interest included St. Erchard's Well, a Gallow Stone, and something called the Peel Ring, Lumphanan. A word jumped out at her.

Macbeth.

Kinny read it, frowned unbelievingly, then read the whole paragraph again.

The Peel Ring of Lumphanan was the location of Macbeth's last stand. In 1057, at a place just a short walk from Kincardine O'Neil, the real Macbeth had died.

❈ ❈ ❈

A TRAIN WHISTLE SOUNDED, high and mournful. Lucas lay sweating in his bed, all the covers thrown off. He had wrestled the window open as far as it would go and had an icy shower afterward, but still he couldn't get cool. It was very late. He desperately wanted to sleep, but images needled at him, strange mixtures of red-and-white gingham, a lumpy Tourist Information bag, ice cream cones that neither he nor Kinny wanted to eat, the scarred wooden handle of a mirror.

What had happened to Kinny in that second-hand shop today? What had happened to him? He had wanted to find that mirror. He had really wanted to find it. It had irritated him that she had found it first, and then it had irritated him that she wouldn't touch it once she did find it. And when he had picked it up himself, that jolt in his mind, like a flash of recognition, or memory — what was it? — and he'd been so unhappy, in despair almost, and there'd been no reason for it, and he hadn't wanted to let Kinny have the mirror at all. He'd forgotten his own reaction when Kinny had acted so strangely, but it came back to him later. Now it wouldn't let him alone.

He turned off his bedside lamp and forced his eyes closed. He had never felt lonely in this room before, and he wouldn't let himself start now. When he was little, he had wished for friends, people you could tell even the dumbest things because you knew they wouldn't make fun of you. But he wasn't little any more. His chest hurt; he wrapped both arms around it and told himself not to be stupid.

Night sounds and smells came in through the window. Flapping wings and rustles in the leaves, the yowling of cats. The smell of tar from the nearby train tracks. A clash of metal as someone shut the gate in the fence out back.

Iron clashing against iron. Swords. A battle.

In the darkness, on the edge of sleep, he thought he was looking in the mirror again. And this time, he remembered....

"You've always said you would help me. Now you tell me to come back tomorrow. Tomorrow! I'll be dead tomorrow, and this country will be dying."

"We prophesied that it would happen, Macbeth."

Certainly they prophesied it. Witches always prophesy. But who listens to prophecies so twisted with double meanings?

They are too busy to help me. They have something to do. That girl, that child all white-blossomed and fresh with her blue-black hair and hungry eyes, what will they do with that girl?

Everything is lost. Fifteen years of peace and prosperity, this green land as young and alive as that girl, and with as many hopes...Oh, Alba, to see you burn under English torches! It is the witches' fault, they could have helped, they promised help, how can they be too busy?

"What will he do, Mother?" The young girl, staring at me like an enemy, whispering.

And the Mother, dismissive. "He can do nothing, child. Macbeth's doom has always been that he must lose to gain. He has lost everything. He must know he can gain nothing more."

Trapped like a bear in a cage, three years of fighting, losing and losing and trying so hard and losing. Friends' bodies burning in the beech grove, pulsing veins that tomorrow would open to soak the earth. The end of everything, trapped as Alba is trapped, as this young girl has been trapped, and these witches to blame, these hideous three. Their fault, nothing to be done, alone and darkness all around....

There were tears on his cheeks. Lucas scrubbed them away. He had been dreaming. He must have been dreaming. That book he'd read at the library today had been all about Macbeth. No wonder he'd dreamed. Trapped. Darkness all around. Alone and trapped.

"I knew it about him," Lucas said angrily into his hot, dark room. "I knew it when I acted him that time on the practice stage."

Trapped like a bear in a cage. History and truth and Shakespeare and lies, and three witches in a dream. And now Jeneva too, falsifying Macbeth in the uniform Montcalm would have worn, with the cross of St. Louis glinting above his cuirass.

Wrong. All wrong.

Not in the legions of horrid hell can come a devil more damned in evils to top Macbeth.

And that, William Shakespeare, was wrong, too.

Lucas closed his eyes again. It took a long, long time, but finally he slept.

Chapter Nine

I T WAS LATE IN THE AFTERNOON. IN Rehearsal Hall 3 the balcony had been hung with long shredded strips of cloth, brown and green, interspersed with twisted metallic shapes. It turned the open area beneath the balcony into something shadowy and strange.

"I didn't know we'd be playing the apparitions scene in a jungle," said the Second Witch, Gwen Park, coming in from the coffee break and seeing it for the first time.

Everett Lunn shrugged his massive shoulders. "Think of it as a cave in a Quebec forest."

"We're trying to put you in the mood, Gwennie," Jeneva said.

Lucas was surprised to see Kinny sitting at the stage manager's table. "I'm going to be the prompter for the rest of today," Kinny greeted him happily. "Jeneva asked me to fill in for Chuck. He went home sick."

Chuck Merensik was one of Everett's two assistants. It was his job to remind the actors of their lines when they began to try to do without their scripts. Prompting was a touchy job, knowing when to jump in with a line and when to allow tense actors some breathing space, and Lucas was a little surprised that Jeneva had decided to let Kinny try it, even if only for a couple of hours. But the play was too heavy a tech job for Everett's other assistant to take over the prompting as well. Lucas hoped Kinny wouldn't get too upset if the actors yelled at her. He hid his concern with a congratulatory grin, giving her the "okay" sign with his right hand. She looked normal enough today, he thought. Maybe he'd overestimated the effect the mirror had had on her yesterday. "What did you do with that mirror we bought?" he asked her, as casually as he could.

Her happy smile faded. "Gave it to Jean," she said shortly.

"Did she like it?"

"Uh huh." She wouldn't look at him. "She's going to check with Jim to see what changes they have to make to it."

She made a show out of opening her script, obviously not wanting to talk any more. So something odd really had happened between her and the mirror yesterday, just as it had with him. He was surprised to find that he was almost jealous.

Brian Able waved a book at him from the side of the hall, and Lucas joined him. He respected Brian for the restrained and imaginative way he was playing Banquo. It was an important role – Macbeth's friend at the beginning of the play, turning suspicious after Duncan's death, then murdered by Macbeth only to come back as a ghost to haunt him. Lucas played all his own scenes in the play with Banquo, first as Fleance, Banquo's son, and later, in the Apparitions Scene, doubling as one of Banquo's ghostly descendants summoned up by the witches to torment Macbeth. Today Brian was free from commitments in other plays, and they were taking advantage of it by scheduling all of Banquo's scenes. That meant that Lucas had been called for most of the day as well.

"Ready, witches?" Everett called. "Alex, you're on, too. We're starting halfway through the scene, when the apparitions come on. Line, please, Kinny."

"'Come high or low,'" Kinny read clearly, "'Thyself and office deftly show.'"

As the scene went on, Lucas was impressed to see that Kinny was a good prompter. She seemed almost instinctively to know the difference between an actor pausing for effect and a genuine loss of memory. Her voice, when she did call a line, was just right, neither diffident nor officious. The actors took her prompts gratifyingly for granted, and Lucas could tell that both Jeneva and Everett were pleased with her.

Jeneva was in a strange mood today, high-spirited and joking between scenes and deeply, physically concentrating during them. Her body seemed to anticipate what the actors were about to do, jerking, twisting in her chair, widening her eyes, licking her lips. Now and then she glided onto the practice stage while people were speaking their lines, moving this actor a millimeter to the right, nodding emphatically at that one, putting both hands on her cheeks in sympathetic sorrow for a third. Earlier, when the witches were tossing horrible things like newt's eyes and a dog's tongue into their cauldron, Jeneva had interrupted and asked Dana, who was supposed to throw a toad into the pot, to kiss the toad once on each cheek first. "The French way, sweetie," she said cheerfully.

She was very pleased with what Alex was doing with Macbeth in this scene. What the others thought about it, Lucas couldn't be sure, but he thought he caught some of his own distaste in Brian's eyes whenever he looked up from his novel to watch. Between them, Jeneva and Alex were turning Macbeth into a kind of soft Marquis de Sade, decadent, aristocratic, self-serving, cowardly, and above all, French. Lucas didn't know very much about General Montcalm, but he was sure he hadn't ruled Quebec the way Jeneva was making Macbeth rule Scotland. She was making up her own history, though she probably would have called it serving her artistic vision.

Adam drifted in on the second run through as the witches began summoning the demonic apparitions from hell. He, like Lucas, was doubling as one of Banquo's eight kingly descendants. "We the only kings here today?" he asked Lucas.

"The rest have other rehearsals," Lucas answered.

"Wish I did," Adam muttered. He caught sight of Norris, who was playing the first apparition with an open cloak draped over his own head, carrying an ostentatiously bleeding fiberglass head wearing a French tricorne. "Woo, catch the big Macker's understudy!" Adam hooted in derision. To Lucas he added, "Bet he wishes Alex would break a leg."

A ghostly woman carried in the second apparition, a baby enveloped in a blood-spattered flag covered with fleurs-de-lis. It was a revolting sight. The third apparition, the crowned youth with a sapling in his hand, seemed tame in comparison. The youth was really an eighteen-year-old woman from the Young Company, short and boyish and with the voice of a ten-year-old. She stumbled on her lines, and Kinny had to correct her.

"Sorry, sorry," the actor said ruefully. "You'd think when you've only *got* one speech...."

She went back to her entrance, got her whole speech out, sank to the floor, and pretended to disappear into it. There would be a trapdoor there, on the real stage.

"You'd better wear kneepads, sweetie," called Jeneva.

"I don't need them."

"We don't want you too bruised to do this again." Jeneva's voice was very firm.

Everett lumbered to his feet and disappeared out the door. He came back carrying knee pads. The actor put them on, her face mutinous.

They repeated the scene. Adam yawned in boredom. Brian read steadily. Finally it was time for the eight kings. Adam and Lucas got up from the table and went to wait in the wings. Brian put a bookmark in his thriller and joined them.

The three witches chanted, "Show his eyes and grieve his heart; come like shadows, so depart."

Brian made his entrance. Adam followed, and then Lucas.

"Where's the last king's mirror?" Dana said. Her voice was low, almost as if she were speaking to herself, but Jeneva heard.

"Lucas needs a mirror, Everett," Jeneva said.

Everett flipped open his red notebook. "Romano's going to be carrying it, not Lucas.

He's not here today."

"It's for the last king in line," Jeneva replied, "and today, that means Lucas. He needs a mirror to hold out to the Thane."

"I'll have something for you tomorrow," Everett said.

"It's confusing for everybody," Jeneva said very clearly, "if we use some props and not others. We've been trying for realism all day, and I'd like to be consistent, if you don't mind."

It had been a long, hot rehearsal, even in the air-conditioned theatre, and people were tired. Six of the eight kings weren't there. There was no way they could get a realistic run-through of this scene today, with the mirror or without it.

"I've got a powder compact," offered the girl with the kneepads.

Jeneva was pursing her lips at Everett.

"I don't know how far Props has got with the mirror," Everett told her. "They were having trouble with it, the last I heard."

"We could run the Apparitions Scene again in the time it'd take you to check," Jeneva said gently.

Everett pushed back his chair and waddled toward the door. "So even God Incarnate gets pushed around now and then," Adam murmured appreciatively.

The kings and Banquo withdrew from the practice stage, and Jeneva began the apparitions scene again. This time the three witches stayed in their balcony-roofed cavern making a slow, weaving, cat-like dance around the cauldron. It was something new, a movement they'd choreographed for themselves. Jeneva scrutinized it intently, frowning a little but not interrupting. It reminded Lucas of winding a watch, passionless and repetitive while the tension grew and grew. He found himself watching the witches rather than the apparitions, mesmerised by the pattern of their dance. The voices of the apparitions, even of Macbeth himself, were mere dronings in the foreground.

A draft seemed to come out of nowhere. The rags hanging from the balcony billowed outward almost horizontally, then flopped back down with an audible rustle. Christine and Gwen hesitated, breaking the pattern of their movement. Dana continued, however. Lucas almost thought she seemed balanced across the cauldron by a fourth figure. He blinked, then started out of his chair. Humpbacked and female...it was the same old woman who had been there when Joan Mackenzie had died! Nobody else seemed to see her; they were all watching Everett come in.

"Got it," Everett said, shutting the door behind him. Lucas tore his gaze from the humpbacked woman. The stage manager had a mirror in his hand. It was the one he and Kinny had found in the second-hand store. He looked at Kinny, at the women by the cauldron. Still four. Why did no one else notice?

"You are a love, Everett," Jeneva said.

"It's not finished," Everett said. "There's a repair to make to the handle, and those things the designer wanted carved...."

"That's all right. It'll do for now." She raised her voice gaily. "Here's your mirror, Lucas."

She expected him to get it from Everett, but he stood frozen. Go, he told himself. But he couldn't. Why was he afraid? He had held the mirror once, even gazed into it, and it hadn't hurt him. If he had imagined seeing things in it, if he'd imagined feeling things, that was no reason not to look in it again. After all, the Macbeth he'd seen there had not been a bad man. So why were his hands trembling? All these people watching, that humpbacked woman....

"Lucas?" Jeneva said a second time.

Everett was walking down the long room toward him, holding out the mirror. He was passing Jeneva's chair now. Lucas felt almost sick. What was wrong with him, for heaven's sake?

"It's very plain wood, isn't it?" Jeneva said. "Let's have a peek."

Everett handed her the mirror. Lucas couldn't help looking at the witches once more. Still four. Gwen and Chrissie were chatting quietly together. How could they, with that disgusting old creature standing right beside them? Was he the only person who could see that something was wrong? His gorge rose; he swallowed hard, closed his eyes tight shut, rubbed his forehead with his sleeve. When he opened his eyes again he saw that Kinny had moved closer to Jeneva. But she wasn't looking at her, she was looking at the area under the balcony, and she had a white, horrified look that Lucas understood very well. So she saw the humpbacked woman too. She saw what he could see — the hump-backed woman and Dana, two very different women concentrating hard on Jeneva with the identical determined, single-minded expression on both their faces.

They're together, Lucas thought with sudden realization. Dana and the humpbacked woman. They're two of a kind. And right now they want something from Jeneva.

"Strangely satisfying," Jeneva said, running her long index finger down the mirror's handle. Her eyes pored over the glass. Was she seeing something in it? Lucas couldn't be sure. It was taking her so long to look up, and he couldn't keep his eyes on her, because there was Dana and the humpbacked woman to look at too, and Kinny, reaching out a shaking hand, too far away to do any good. And still Jeneva stared into the glass. Lucas felt sweat pooling in his armpits, behind his knees, between his toes, in the creases of his eyelids. Why didn't anyone else notice what was happening here?

It seemed hours before Jeneva lifted her eyes from the mirror. Her expression was guarded, but showing none of the dazed panic Kinny had exhibited after looking in the mirror in the antique shop. Had she seen something or hadn't she? Lucas sent a quick glance to the witches. Three again. The humpbacked woman was gone. His shoulders sagged. Was it over, then? Was that all that was going to happen?

Jeneva held the mirror out to Everett. "I like it the way it is," she said calmly. "I think we should change our minds about decorating it. It's ideal for Quebec in 1759. I don't even want the gouge in the handle fixed. Make a note to tell Jim, will you, Everett?"

Everett scribbled in his notebook, then took the mirror. And then he was handing it to Lucas. There was nothing he could do but take it. He grasped it gingerly with two fingertips and a thumb and waited, but nothing happened, except that Dana was observing him with the same marble-hard eyes she had just focussed on Jeneva.

She wanted him to look into the mirror. She wanted to see his reaction to it. Lucas didn't know how he knew, but he was sure he was right.

"The mirror's not made of eggshells, Lucas," Jeneva said, quirking a brow at his tentative fingers.

He didn't know how it happened. His palm closed convulsively around the handle. He hadn't meant to look, but his eyes lowered, pulled, it seemed, by the blue sheen of mirror glass. And then a full moon shone out at him over a jagged ring of standing stones, and he was in it, he was *there*, he was someone else, and oh, he was glad, glad. Only the gladness dimmed too fast, and there was a sound in the Goddess Ring, Words of Power in a young girl's voice....

Light flares, brilliantly blue. The girl keeps her eyes shut tight. When the light dies down she opens them, hungry little cat-like slits. "Is it...done? Am I Maiden?"

The Mother shows her teeth. It might be a smile. "Not yet. You must say it twice more. Once to awaken, once to open, and once, last of all, to seal. You have only awakened the Power. The rest remains."

"And afterward, the Power shall be mine."

Alba is dying, and this girl is destroying herself. Christ of the Culdees, where are you?

She peers into the glass. Frowning proudly, she speaks the Words again. "Two into one. Find through this glass a past for thy future, that the name of the Goddess be not forgotten."

A second blue flash, brighter than the first. This time the girl squints throughout it, concentrating on the glass. "I see her! She waits for the third time, when I will join her. And then —"

"Then you will be Maiden. In your body will be all the Power of the Three."

The girl smiles. She smiles!

"Two into one," *she begins again, the final time.*

Stop it. Have to stop it. No time to plan. Just do it. This first. And this. The girl shrieking. This is for you, stop it, you'll see it's for the best, stop. One of the witches curled on the ground. Gagging noises. The other clawing, then on her back. The looking glass, quick. Now, yes, hands on the mirror, now!

"Two into one! Find through this glass a future for thy past, that the name of Macbeth be not forgotten!"

Light! Eyes and hand, burning, burning, the handle, he must let go....

"Lucas! He's out like a light. Is somebody calling the doctor? Lucas!"

"Is he coming round?"

Lucas blinked up from the floor of the practice stage at Stratford. "What's the matter? My hand hurts."

Someone took the mirror from him, opening his fingers gently. "God, look at it. His palm's almost raw. How did you do it, Lucas?"

"I..." He swallowed, licked his lips, tried to think. His skull throbbed; so did his hand. Think. Don't say anything. Just think.

"Somebody get him a drink of water."

He got down one mouthful, two. His brain was clearer. What he said now would matter. These people were superstitious. They would be perfectly ready to believe the truth, if he told them. And then they would be so afraid of the mirror they would never want it around them again. Jeneva would have to get rid of it. She might have to get rid of him, too.

It wasn't the mirror's fault his hand had been hurt. It was because of what he'd done — what Macbeth had done — while holding the mirror. For a moment the thought of Macbeth filled him with gladness, the same gladness he had first felt on looking into the mirror again. And then the horror afterward. He wanted to know more about that. He wanted to know everything about it. And without that mirror he was doomed never to discover another thing.

Invent something. Quick.

"I hurt my hand at lunch. I was helping haul in a boat at the river. Got rope burn when I slipped on the grass."

"You should have dealt with it." Everett sounded almost angry. "We've got first aid kits."

"Really, Lucas," Jeneva said, "all you had to do was hold the mirror in your other hand. Why you men must act as if you're indestructible...." She shook her head exasperatedly.

"The ambulance is on its way," Adam

announced breathlessly, running into the hall.

"Cancel it." Lucas scrambled to his feet. "I mean, thanks, but really, I'm fine." He smiled, flexed his hand at them, and through the stabbing pain somehow kept the smile on his face. He saw Kinny wince, and knew that she, at least, hadn't been fooled.

"I'll get someone to bandage it," Everett said.

"I can do it myself. I'll take care of it as soon as I get back to my B&B." It was hard work, smiling like this. He didn't know when he'd been so tired.

Jeneva said, "Skip along there now, Lucas. It's almost six, anyway. I think we'll all call it a day." She smiled cheerily around at the cast, but her lips were pale, the lipstick chewed off. There was something else different about her, but Lucas was in no shape to analyze what it was. "I'm pleased with all your hard work today," she said to everyone impartially. "It's really starting to pay off. I'll have notes for you in the morning, but just for tonight, take it easy. Kinny, you did a great job this afternoon. If Chuck is still sick tomorrow, will you prompt for us again?"

"Sure," Kinny said. But her voice was joyless, almost vague. And she was looking, not at Jeneva, but at Dana Sloe's blank, inward-looking face.

"Be here at ten, just in case," Jeneva told her.

"The rest of you, check the call sheets as usual."

It all sounded very normal. Lucas made for the door. Maybe people actually had believed his crazy story about getting a rope burn at lunch. But then he noticed that Adam didn't quite return his goodbye nod, and Christine was whispering furtively to Gwen. He heard something about "this play," and a single other word, "cursed." There was going to be trouble there, all right. Everett Lunn was glaring accusingly at the mirror on the table in front of him. And Kinny's gaze was still riveted on Dana Sloe, and now there was an angry, determined flash to her wide green eyes.

Trouble there, too.

Lucas straightened his shoulders, gave the room one last, wide, smile, and strode casually out. It was one of the best bits of acting he had ever done. The worst of it was, he didn't think it convinced anyone at all.

Chapter Ten

"WHAT HAPPENED TO HIM, DANA?"
They were outside the theatre,
just the two of them. It wasn't
quite dark, but already the moon was rising.
Kinny had waited for Dana in the parking
lot near the stage door. It had taken a long
time.

"What? Oh, hello, Kinny." The other
woman peered at her as if she were very far
away. Her long pale hair was messy. There were
deep lines etched around her mouth that Kinny
hadn't noticed before. She blinked her round
pale eyes at Kinny with the tired, distracted air
of someone who had been working very hard.
"Were you saying something?"

"I asked you what happened to Lucas."
Kinny's voice was trembling. Now that it came
down to it, she was no longer at all sure she was
doing the right thing.

"What happened to him? He passed out.
You saw as much as I did. Why are you asking
me?"

Dana's eyes were no longer vague. Instead
they had gone as bright and hard as marbles.
They looked just the way they had when Jeneva

had been holding the mirror and Dana had been looking at her. And Dana had not been alone, watching Jeneva like that. There had been another woman with her, a woman with demanding silver eyes. Kinny had seen her, and so had Lucas.

"I saw her, Dana," Kinny said. "The old woman with the hump. She's been watching me ever since I came to Stratford, and finally I saw her. She was with you in there."

"What?" Dana sounded indifferent.

"What? Is that all you have to say? She wasn't there, and then...she was. How did she do that? You know. I know you know. Who is she, Dana? Was she the one who hurt Lucas's hand?" She stopped then, shaking all over.

"That was a rope burn, he said."

Kinny took a deep breath, then let it out again. She knew that Lucas had lied about the rope burn. After she'd told him Jeneva had asked her to prompt, he had made a circle with the thumb and index finger of his right hand, and there had been nothing wrong with his palm then at all. "He may have said it, but it's not true."

Abruptly and decisively, Dana turned away. "Come," she said. She didn't wait to see if Kinny followed. By the time Kinny got her wits together enough to run after her, she was already halfway down the parking lot. In the twilight she seemed an amorphous shape, not at all solid. She moved with a fluid kind of grace that surprised Kinny, who had always thought of the older woman as awkward, almost ugly. She turned to the right outside the parking lot and headed downhill toward the river, Kinny still a few steps behind. There was no one on the street, not even a passing car. When they got to the riverbank, it too was oddly deserted. Everything seemed dim, empty of colour and life. Dana went to the very edge of the water, then stopped as abruptly as she had started. Kinny joined her. Neither of them said anything for some time.

There was no wind. The river was glassy. A white swan, still as a cutout, floated on top of its own reflection. A silvery half-moon drifted beside it. When Dana finally spoke it was in a dreamy, soft voice that was totally unlike her. Her eyes were on the river. She might almost have been speaking to herself.

"Water is an ancient power, water like this, still water that absorbs and reflects and is linked to a place and seems all surface. But it is not only a surface; it has depths that cannot be fathomed from outside. It must be entered to give up its secrets.

"That looking glass, too. It is no more all on the surface than is truth or this water. Only a few people recognize that. People who can see beneath the surface of that looking glass are the people who need to. They are also those who may, perhaps, be needed themselves. There are rewards for seeing, as you may learn. There may, as well, be prices to pay. It knows what you must do in return."

Kinny shivered. "I don't care about me. It's Lucas. Dana, I have to know. Is that mirror dangerous for him?"

"All the ancient powers are dangerous to those who do not understand them. It is like water. Some people can swim in it, some immerse themselves and drown." Her voice was soft, calm as the river, mesmerising. "You want to help Lucas. You are worried about him. You think his reaction to the mirror is your responsibility."

Inexplicably, Kinny wanted her to understand. "Well, you see, it was my idea to shop for a mirror. If it hadn't been for me, Props would have made one, and nobody at the theatre would have seen that mirror at all. And then, Lucas came shopping with me that day. He saw it when I did...."

"You feel responsible. It is the kind of person you are. You need to feel responsible, you need to help people. That is one of your truths."

The moonlight, the still river, the dulcet singsong voice...I'm in a dream, Kinny thought,

I'm asleep. None of this is real. But Lucas's burned hand had been real, and the strangely old, bitter twist to his lips as he opened his eyes on the practice stage floor, and those eyes themselves, seeking out the mirror again, afraid and desirous and evasive all at the same time.

"Who are you really, Dana? Why are you here?"

At this, Dana turned away from her survey of the river and looked straight at Kinny. Her eyes were huge, silver as the moon. "Me? I'm just the First Witch, a small part of the Scottish play. As for you, well...Lucas has been hurt. You want to help him. You can help him. But help has its price. Power has its price. Something, or somebody, always has to pay."

"Do you mean — me?"

Dana said nothing. Her eyes glowed. Kinny stared into them. Her own reflection stared back. Hair loose and flowing and woven with hawthorn, berry-lush skin, beautiful.... *You will be Maiden. You will have my power.*

"No," Kinny breathed. "No."

"What is owed must be paid. That is one of the oldest truths."

"I don't owe anything."

"Do you not? Are you sure? You have many things to learn, Kincardine O'Neil. But it has begun. At last it has begun."

OVER THE NEXT WEEK, Kinny watched Lucas, and knew that he had changed. He'd never been very friendly with the rest of the company, but people talked to him, and listened to him, and whether they liked him well or not they seemed to take it for granted that he was part of the group. Now he didn't seem to want any of that. He was polite, and he even smiled now and then, but both the smile and the politeness was forced. Kinny had thought of him as the sort of person who tried to be kind whatever his mood, unless he thought someone was being deliberately cruel or small-minded, or if he was embarrassed, as he must have been when she saw him doing Macbeth's soliloquy in the empty rehearsal hall.

Now he wasn't kind to anyone. It wasn't that he was unkind. It was just that he didn't seem to notice other people at all.

In a way it was just as well. Other people were avoiding him. Christine had started it, talking about curses and the Scottish play and reminding people that no one had noticed Lucas' injured hand until after that incident in rehearsal. Not everyone paid attention, but Norris did, and Jon Crowell who played Macduff, and a few people in Wardrobe and Props, and some of the older actors. Little by little people began to be in other places when Lucas appeared, or were busily reading or making notes when he sat down at the table beside them. He'd had a badly-explained accident in a bad-luck play, and people were afraid his ill-luck might be catching.

Kinny wanted to talk to him about the mirror, but she didn't know how. There was no opportunity, anyway. She never saw him except in rehearsal. He arrived at Rehearsal Hall 3 every day at ten o'clock whether he was called or not, and stayed until they broke for the day, unless he had a costume fitting or a fight rehearsal in another hall or a performance at one of the other theatres. On breaks he slipped out quickly, and alone; Kinny didn't know where he went, but he was always back when the rehearsal resumed. When he had any acting to do he did it cursorily; and when he wasn't on, he just watched. She noticed how intently he scrutinized Alexander Blair's every move as Macbeth, and how often he frowned. Once, looking up a word for Jeneva in the dictionary they kept on the research table, she had to pass Lucas, and she could hear him muttering one of Macbeth's speeches, staring burningly at Alex, "O, full of scorpions is my mind...."

Kinny was still prompting at every rehearsal, though Chuck Merensik had been back at work for almost a week. Jeneva had asked her to keep on with the prompting so that Chuck could help Everett's other assistant with the tech work. Kinny was helping Jeneva in other ways, too. She got things from Jeneva's office, marked particular pages in the books they kept on a table in the rehearsal hall, and bought snacks for production meetings and rehearsals. More and more she felt herself a part of things. A couple of weeks ago that would have made her very happy, but now she hardly noticed.

They hadn't rehearsed with the mirror again, not since last Tuesday. It hadn't been necessary, because they weren't running the Apparitions Scene again, until today. Even today they wouldn't be using the antique mirror. On Wednesday, the morning after Lucas' blackout, Jim Simpson from Props had whisked blithely into the rehearsal hall carrying a child's hand mirror, pink, with a Barbie Doll painted on the back. "Rehearsal mirror," he'd announced cheerfully, taking the other one from the shelf beside the practice stage. "Got to keep this one safe, Jeneva tells me. Not that it's any great beauty. I'd fix that handle, whatever Jeneva says, if I didn't have more than enough to do already, now my chief leaf-sewer's gone."

He'd smiled at Kinny who had been sitting over her script. She had smiled back, but a little uneasily, seeing the ancient mirror resting so casually in his palm. "I could come in after rehearsal and do some leaves for you," she offered.

"You'd give your last five minutes on this earth to help your worst enemy," Jim had said. "No, no, thanks, lovebug, but no. You need some time to yourself. We'll get it done."

Now it was Tuesday again. After lunch, for the first time in a week, they would be rehearsing the scene that had led to Lucas' injury. Probably it was because of that that Lucas seemed especially on edge all morning. He kept getting up from his stool, going over to the research table and glancing absentmindedly through books on eighteenth century warfare; or pouring cups of coffee he then forgot to drink. Whatever restless wandering course he took, Kinny noticed that he always avoided Dana Sloe. She guessed he too knew that Dana wasn't just an ordinary actor. It was another bond between them, along with the mirror. And still she couldn't talk to him.

Lucas wasn't the only one to avoid Dana. Kinny did it too, as much as she could, though for some reason she didn't feel good about it. Breakfasts were the worst. Dana would sit there sipping coffee and eating bacon and listening as Kinny made conversation with Andrew about movies or music videos or the latest theatre gossip. Her round eyes would look at Kinny with the same calm, assessing under-standing as on that evening by the river when she had said, "You need to feel responsible, you need to help people," but there was sorrow there, too, almost a kind of yearning. That other pair of eyes, the cold, demanding ones that Kinny had first seen the day Joan Mackenzie had died, had completely stopped watching her. It was as if they didn't need to any more, as if they were somehow surer of her.

It was lunch time now, and Dana had gone out, along with all the other actors. Kinny and Chuck Merensik were the only people in the rehearsal hall. Chuck was setting up the props for the first scene after lunch, and Kinny was making a note of the lines the actors kept get-ting wrong. "You doing anything special tonight, Kinny?" Chuck asked her. He was a rumpled, good-natured sheepdog of a man in his late twenties. To Kinny's astonishment, he seemed to have taken an interest in her.

"Going to Jean's for supper," she said.

"Too bad. I was wondering if you'd come swimming with me at the quarry in St. Mary's. Maybe another time?"

"Why not?" she said, smiling.

He was nice, but somehow she was going to have to tell him she was only sixteen. After see-ing herself in the mirror, all skinny and stretched and ugly in that ponytail, she had begun to wear her hair looser now, and even to herself she looked better. Her green eyes seemed much bigger and brighter, and her mouth, instead of being just too wide, generous and soft.

"Innocently sultry," Adam had said, approvingly, and, "You want to watch out you don't go and get sexy on us, Kinny-my-love."

There was no doubt about it. People weren't treating her like a kid any more. Even Lucas wasn't treating her like a kid. Before, he'd done things like protecting her from Adam's curiosity and taking her out for ice cream, the kind of thing a really nice person would do for someone young and a little bit lonely. Now, he was treating her just the same as everybody else.

Chuck adjusted the position of the cauldron under the overhanging balcony, then waved at Kinny and left for lunch. She had brought a sandwich, and ate it at her table while finishing her notes. Afterward she decided to go and ask Jean what she could bring to supper that night.

There was a meeting going on in Soft Props, but Jean wasn't there. Kinny went on to the large Carpentry and Steel Workshop. At first she thought no one was in the room at all, but then she saw a flicker of movement behind some metal shelving that jutted halfway into the room from the side wall. The movement stopped. Kinny frowned. Whoever it was back there was being awfully quiet. Just standing there, it looked like. Kinny was almost certain it wasn't Jean, but she was curious now. She went farther into the room, almost tiptoeing, stopped, and then went farther. She was at the end of the half-wall of shelving, now. The person behind it was still making no noise at all. Kinny leaned forward and peeked around the shelving.

There were two people, not one, back there. Farthest away was Lucas. He was in profile, facing the shelves that contained finished props, and he was holding one of the props in both his hands. It was the antique hand mirror. He held it straight out in front of him, staring into the glass, elbows locked, each palm cupping one curved wooden side, the handle projecting below. Clearly he was riveted by whatever it was that he saw. He had no idea anyone else was there. But someone was. And that someone was Jeneva Strachan.

It was amazing that she could have got so close without Lucas becoming aware of her. She was only a few steps away from him. Her head was tilted at a sharp angle, her body stretched upward and to the side, apparently trying to peer over Lucas' outstretched arm into whatever scene he was watching in the glass. From the taut muscles of her long neck to the straining leather sole of one balled foot, her entire body spoke of strain and rigid control. No burglar could have been more furtive. She had every right to be there, looking at the props for her own play, but no one observing her as Kinny did now would have thought so.

She certainly didn't want Lucas to know she was there. Was she spying on him? Had she noticed, as Kinny had, that something was wrong with him this week? And if she got a good look at that mirror and saw — as most people would see — nothing there except Lucas' own reflection, would she start thinking that more things were wrong with him than she'd thought?

Silently Kinny withdrew behind the shelving. She's my boss, she told herself unhappily. She's got a right to keep an eye on her actors. But Lucas was her friend. Lost like that in whatever dark and magnetic vision he saw in that glass, he was vulnerable. Kinny couldn't just leave him there staring while Jeneva watched him and wondered.

She tiptoed back to the door of the workshop, then called in what she hoped was an ordinary tone, "Jean? Hey, Jean, are you in here?"

Hardly an eye-blink passed before Jeneva appeared at the end of the half-wall of shelving. Fast, Kinny thought. If it took Lucas a second or two to come out of it, he might not even know Jeneva had been near him.

"Jean's not here, Kinny," Jeneva said. "I'm looking for her or Jim myself. But Lucas seems to be the only warm body here." Her voice was so natural it was impossible not to believe her.

Shoulders back and arms straight at his sides, Lucas came out. Jeneva moved slightly away from him. He tried to smile at her. "I was just checking out Fleance's drum-strap," he said. "I think it's a little long for me."

"I see." Jeneva gave him a cool look. "Tell Jim about it, will you?" She turned to Kinny. "Had your lunch yet, sweetheart?"

"Yes."

"Good. We'll be starting up again in a few minutes. I'd better go see if I can have Jim paged."

She left. Kinny stood gazing at Lucas. After a moment he came over to her. "What I was really doing was looking at that mirror we found," he said defiantly.

"I know. I saw you. So did Jeneva. She was right beside you, until I called out."

"I didn't notice her."

"You didn't notice anything, except that mirror."

He was silent, defensive, curled up within himself. He wasn't going to say anything more about the mirror unless she did first.

"Lucas, the other day — you know, the day we were in the secondhand store — I saw something weird in that mirror."

He blinked at her. "What did you see?"

She took a deep breath. He was the only person she could talk to, the only person besides Dana who might be able to help her make sense of it. And she couldn't talk to Dana.

"Well, first there was moonlight, and some stones. Like Stonehenge, sort of, only smaller. There was an old woman in the stones holding a mirror. I think it was our mirror. The one we found in the store, I mean." She paused, gulped, began again. "The old woman was with two other women, and a girl. They were doing something with the mirror. Something weird. A man came then. He was really angry, and something awful happened. Then I...well, I guess I woke up, sort of. Is that anything like what you saw, Lucas? I know you saw something."

He was silent for so long she wondered if he even remembered she was there. Then, in a voice so low she had to strain to hear it, he said, "Did you ever look into the mirror again?"

"I didn't want to. I didn't like it. I kept getting other people's feelings —"

"Whose feelings?" He shot the question at her, so sharp and intense it confused her.

"I...listen, Lucas, I'm telling you everything,

and you're not saying anything. It's you who —"

"You did look again into the mirror, didn't you? Even if you didn't want to?"

She heaved an impatient sigh. "Later that night. It was an accident. The paper came loose. I didn't mean to look."

"What did you see? The same thing? What?"

"Just...a girl." She wouldn't tell him who the girl was. "What about you? You've been looking into that mirror a lot, haven't you? Do you see the same things every time you look, or —"

He was shaking his head. "I don't want to talk about it."

"Why not? I told you what I saw. Why won't you tell me?"

"What about the next time you looked? Did you see that man again? The man you said was really angry?"

"I never looked again. I told you, I didn't want to."

"You might see him, if you did look again. Come on, I'll go with you. We'll look in it together."

She shook her head, backing away. "It's you who's got a problem with it now, not me."

He grabbed for her and caught her arm. "I want you to."

"Why?"

"Because."

"I won't see anything," she said.

A strange, dull certainty had hold of her. She wouldn't see anything. Not this time. She knew it.

"Then why don't you want to look?"

She went still, his hand gripping her arm. "All right," she said at last. "But I'm going to do it alone."

He dropped her arm. She walked slowly over to the half-wall of shelving. Lucas followed her, pausing where she had stopped earlier, letting her go alone to the shelf where the mirror lay face-down. She picked it up, turned it over and made herself look.

She had been right. There was nothing at all unusual in the mirror, only some shelving, a hanging warehouse light, and in the middle, her own ordinary face.

Not like that other time, when she had been so beautiful, and someone had asked her what she wanted. Out loud she had denied that she wanted anything, but what went on in her mind had been very different. She'd wished to be allowed to work for Jeneva. And now she was working for Jeneva. She'd wished to be really good at what she did so people would respect her. She'd wished they would stop treating her like a kid. And now people thought she was a good prompter, and relied on her, and no one was treating her like a kid at all. And she'd wished that she would stop seeing things in this mirror. And she had. That silent wish had come true, just like all the others.

Kinny stared at the mirror. It couldn't be. Wishes granted! It was the stuff of fairy tales. Things like that just didn't happen.

She didn't even want them to happen.

She could test it out, of course. She had the means right here. All she had to do was wish to see something of those strange events in the mirror again. If it didn't happen — and it wouldn't, she didn't want it to, the whole idea was crazy — she'd know she'd been imagining things, she'd know it was all just a coincidence.

But if it did happen....

It wouldn't.

She wished.

And the mirror fogged over, and again it cleared, and Kinny saw a girl with blue-black hair. There was a hand holding a mirror, another hand arranging hawthorn blossoms in the girl's hair.

I wished, and it happened, she told herself. She put the mirror down and blindly walked away.

Chapter Eleven

ALL THAT HOT SUMMER SATURDAY THE riverbank had been packed with tourists bargain-hunting at a local craft fair, but now dusk was settling in, and a lot of the booths and card-tables were gone. Lucas stopped at a table where a girl in glasses was taking chains and earrings off her peg-board. "I like that one," he said, pointing to a pendant hanging on a thick-linked iron chain. The pendant was a circular piece of metal with sixteen smaller circles carved around the edge and five men carved in the centre. The sixteen circles depicted men, stylized animals, abstract designs, and something that looked like a snowflake.

"It's Celtic," the girl said, "a replica from the time of Alfred the Great. The symbols stand for reason and memory and the will to make choices. Want to try it on? It's iron, not silver, but it feels good."

He put the heavy iron chain over his head. "Next to your skin," the girl ordered.

Obediently he shoved it under his shirt. It was cool against his chest. He liked the idea that more than a thousand years ago men had believed in reason and free will. "I'll take it," he said.

The girl smiled. "You need a bag?"

"I'll wear it."

He left the girl packing up, and wandered aimlessly down to the water's edge. It was getting dark. Already the moon was up, shining in the mirror-smooth surface of the river. A canoeist was paddling hurriedly upriver under the arched wooden bridge that led to the island. Drips from his paddle glittered in the moonlight; swirls in the water showed where the canoe cut it. Lucas looked at his watch. Still more than an hour to kill before he had to go back to the theatre for his last act entrance in *Romeo and Juliet.*

Normally he stayed in his dressing room after the first act because it was too much trouble to get out of his costume and back in again, but tonight he was too restless to sit and read. He'd spent the day watching the *Macbeth* rehearsals. The production was smoothing out. Jeneva was happy. Even the actors seemed moderately pleased. Lucas had seen it before, the way working hard on even the most worthless productions eventually made you believe in them. Next week the show would be moving to the real stage upstairs. Usually that was exciting, but Lucas dreaded it. A set built for Quebec in 1759 would merely underline the falseness that made this production worse for Lucas with each passing day.

It was harder because Lucas was getting to know the real Macbeth. He might have been afraid to look in the mirror after his hand had been burned, but he wasn't. He had figured out that he'd been burned because he'd held the handle the way Macbeth had when he grabbed it from the witch and uttered the spell that put an end to her designs on that young girl. Now Lucas held the mirror by the sides, and no matter how many times he looked into it it didn't burn him again. It didn't show him anything new, though. Every time he went to the mirror he saw the same scene, and every time he saw it he liked Macbeth more. He was the kind of man Lucas had never imagined to exist, an honourable man who knew what it was to be alone and yet had friends he cared about, a man with deep and hard-held principles he could throw away when it came to a choice between them and something that mattered more. Yet every day Lucas had to go to rehearsals of a play about him, a production that was false to the man in every way. It wasn't even true to the man Shakespeare had written, and that was false enough. The sole authentic thing in Jeneva's whole production was the mirror, and he and Kinny seemed to be the only people who knew it.

Lucas didn't discuss the mirror with her. It

wasn't because she wouldn't believe him. She said she had stopped seeing things in the mirror now, but at least she *had* seen them. What she'd seen had been much the same as the things he saw, though less detailed. She didn't even know that the man who had come to the witches was Macbeth. That was one reason Lucas didn't talk things over with her. She knew less than he did. The other was that, unlike him, she didn't want to know more.

It never bored him that he always saw the same sequence of events as he had that first time, but still he wished he could see more. What had happened before Macbeth had come to the witches for help against Malcolm? What had happened after Macbeth had altered the witches' spell? Why had those few small changes made him burn his hand so badly that Lucas had burned his, too, reliving the experience?

Find through this glass a future for thy past, that the name of Macbeth be not forgotten!

The young girl had been supposed to say, "a past for thy future," meaning that the spirit of the aging Hag could enter her own young body. Macbeth had changed the words "past" and "future" around. Obviously he had meant that to make the Hag older, the exact opposite of what the witches wanted. His intervention must have sent the Hag into the future sometime. The mirror would have gone too because she was inside it. But what had happened to her after that? And what had happened to Macbeth?

It had gotten dark while he stood thinking; the streetlamps were on, and all the booths were gone from the park. Lucas checked his watch. He couldn't miss his entrance in *Romeo and Juliet*'s last act. As Balthasar he had to bring Romeo the news of Juliet's supposed death. He had eleven lines in that scene. To miss a cue at any time was unthinkable; in front of a live audience it would be unforgivable. But he still had a few minutes. He began jogging along the manicured river-bank toward the bridge. Once round the island and then the four blocks to the theatre — that would get his blood moving.

He was in the shadow of a willow tree when he saw Dana Sloe. She was hurrying down the road from the Festival Theatre, moving fast. In the glow from the street-lamps Lucas watched her approach. She looked worried. She came to the river and headed at once for the bridge to the island. Something about her face reminded Lucas of how she'd stared at him the day he'd burned his hand, and how she and that hunchbacked woman had seemed to be working together.

Lucas glanced worriedly at his watch, but he had to find out where she was going in such a hurry and with that look on her face. Only five minutes, he told himself, just enough to see what she's up to. He too headed for the bridge, keeping out of the light in case she should look back. She didn't. She was on the island now, disappearing into the huge trees that made the island a favourite spot for picnickers. Lucas hesitated before stepping onto the bridge himself. He would be outlined against the sky there; she could be watching him from the shadows without his knowing it. The thought made him feel queasy. Stupid, he accused himself, it's a public place, I've got as much right to be here as she does.

His five minutes were almost up. Quickly and quietly he slipped across the bridge. There were no lights on the island, and in the shadow of the trees he could see almost nothing. He stumbled into a flower bed, recovered, and forced himself to stop. More noise would alert Dana, and he didn't have time to deal with her questions if she caught him. He was about to turn back when a voice came out of the darkness.

"Are you there?"

Dana's voice. Lucas' heart pounded. Was she talking to him?

"Of course. Did you communicate with our Sister?" Another voice, harsher, impatient.

He stood perfectly still. The hunchback. It had to be.

"She won't let us just take it and go." Dana's

voice again. "There is time, she says. Things are working the way she wants. She says she has a plan."

"We know all about that."

"Not all. There's more. She's...been too long a prisoner."

Silence. Then, "She knows about the boy?"

"He's part of it."

"I wonder...."

In the thoughtful pause that followed, Lucas raised his wrist to his eyes. His watch was fluorescent; he almost groaned when he saw the time. Less than twenty minutes to his entrance, and he wasn't even in costume! There was no time to think. He tore out of the flower bed and dashed for the bridge, his feet thudding on the grass. The glimmer of water was just ahead. There was a noise behind him. He sprinted onto the bridge, thundering across the wooden planking with his heart pounding in his ears and a hot circle of pain hanging just over his heart. The medallion. His fingers closed around it, shirt and all; one last flying leap and he was on the river-bank. He was going to make it.

And when he got himself on stage, with his costume awry and only a moment after Romeo had given him his cue, he could feel the medallion under his Montague colours, and it wasn't hot any more, but iron-cold and strong, like armour.

※ ※ ※

"TAKE TEN DOWN TO TWENTY, 103 down to five. Go."

The Festival Theatre was almost completely in darkness. The stage was dimly lit, but in the house just two lights burned, and these had been set up to shine only on the tables where the stage manager and the lighting designer were working. Kinny had to feel her way to a seat. In the air-conditioned darkness, so unlike the brightly lit rehearsal hall, excitement prickled inside her. She knew she wasn't the only one to feel it. In less than an hour Jeneva's revival of *Macbeth* was going to be rehearsed on the real stage for the very first time.

"Something warmer, Ingrid?" Jeneva's voice. Now that Kinny's eyes were getting used to the gloom she could see her, erect beside the hunched shape of Ingrid Hanna, the lighting designer.

Ingrid spoke into her head-set microphone. "Show me 102 on-stage. Take 103 out...good." On stage the pale light changed tone, pinkish instead of blue. Kinny thought of dawn.

"Next cue," Jeneva said.

Inside his tiny pool of light Everett was scribbling in his little red notebook and speaking into his headset at the same time. On stage the pink light grew harsher. "That works,"

Jeneva said. "Maybe even up a bit. Cue sound, Everett." A short pause, followed by a discordant few bars of a song Kinny felt she ought to recognize, but didn't.

"Wipe to coincide with sound."

Blackout.

It was all coming together. The lighting plot, the sound cues, the set, probably the costumes, too, though Kinny hadn't seen them yet. She thought of the weeks in the rehearsal hall downstairs; of coloured tape on the floor that her mind had turned into solid walls and trees and stairs; of actors in ordinary clothes who had somehow started growing other people inside them. And now the actors and those hundreds of other people working on *Macbeth* outside the rehearsal hall would be coming together, bringing their combined arts to bear on a great play whose director had decided it must do something Shakespeare had never intended. It was strange and sad, Kinny thought, to want it to work and hope it would fail, both at the same time.

"Onstage, please, Ladies and Gentlemen. Full company, please, onstage." Everett's voice echoed through the house and into the speakers of the corridors and dressing-rooms outside. He flipped a switch, and his ordinary voice added, "House lights to half."

As the light grew Kinny took stock of the

theatre. It was its sheer size that impressed her most. There seemed to be thousands of seats. Kinny counted eleven separate aisles, all descending steeply from the lobby level and sectioning the auditorium like an orange. The stage itself seemed small and plain, just a simple wooden platform with its own balcony, a few pillars, a staircase. Entrances were mostly behind the wooden backdrop, but there were two steep runways as well that went directly under the audience.

In her week in Props, Kinny had learned from Jean that productions here usually had fairly simple sets. "Almost no walls," she had said. "We use banners and tapestries instead. And furniture, of course. Heavy-looking and elaborate for wealthy houses, simple stuff for the plebes. We've got a lovely English campaign table for Malcolm to sit at when Macduff visits him. Just the sort of thing Wolfe would have used on the Plains of Abraham in 1759."

The opening set had neither tapestries nor furniture. There was a new stone-like edging to the balcony. Some nearly-invisible netting hung from it, woven with moss-covered branches and lichens. It hung down low enough that it made a cave out of the area below the balcony, and looked a lot more real than the brown and green rags of rehearsal. At stage right was a copse of weedy-looking pine trees. A few realistic looking rocks sat at stage left. Dominating center stage was the huge maple tree Kinny had last seen in the corridor downstairs, now incorporating the central pillar that supported the balcony. 21,500 leaves. Kinny marvelled. Jim had been right. It looked so real she almost couldn't believe she had helped to make it.

In twos and threes the actors came out on stage. Christine came in from stage left with Gwen and Dana. The assorted lords of Scotland entered behind them in an awkward clump. Jon Crowell jogged in wearing tennis shorts and stained old Reeboks. Meredith Archer and Alex Blair came in together. Lucas entered on his own behind them, looking very stern.

He seemed thinner these days, and desperately unhappy. Kinny thought acting had once meant a lot to him, but now he went through his role of Fleance like a sleepwalker. She wasn't the only one who noticed. In one rehearsal during the stabbing of Banquo, Jeneva had stopped everyone to address him coldly. "Lucas, that man's dying, and he's your father, and you look as if you're adding numbers in your head."

Lucas had flushed, and when they went back to the scene he'd acted it brilliantly. In the break he'd actually said something about it to Kinny. "The whole play's going to hell anyway. Why should any of us bit players care about being true to our characters when Jeneva and Alex have destroyed the most important role in the play?"

Kinny could understand how he felt. If the falseness of Alex's portrayal of Macbeth was ruining the play for Lucas, the anti-French-Canadian bigotry was ruining it for her. But *she* wasn't losing weight, or only half-doing her job, or staring at everyone with burning, angry eyes. Obviously much more was wrong with Lucas than just Jeneva's manipulation of the play.

It was the mirror, Kinny was sure. He was still going down to Props and staring into it every chance he got. She had followed him as far as the door of the Props Room a few times, though she couldn't make herself go farther. But she knew what he was doing behind the half-wall of shelving. It was what he saw in the shiny blue glass back there that was eating him up inside. He was immersing himself in its power the way Dana had said, and it was drowning him.

She had tried to warn him, running openly after him one day after rehearsal when she had known he was on his way to the mirror. "It's dangerous, Lucas. It hurt you once. It can do worse than that, if you keep looking in it."

"It's not dangerous, Kinny, it's —"

"What?"

He only looked at her with a strange mixture of uncertainty and pity. Then he'd gone on to the mirror anyway. He was obsessed with it, like an alcoholic with a bottle. Kinny had felt sick, watching him go and remembering that it had been she who had suggested buying a mirror in the first place. With all her heart she wished she could figure out some way of helping him.

She had told no one about the wishes she had made into the mirror, though she thought incessantly about what had happened. Four wishes, five counting the one she'd made as a kind of test, and all of them had come true. She had spent most of the last week trying to figure out a reasonable, unmagical explanation for it. The best she could come up with was coincidence. It wasn't much of an explanation.

She stared at the actors on stage, at the backstage crew bustling about. She had thought herself one of them, but now she didn't know. If they'd only changed toward her because of some kind of magical compulsion, what did any of their new respect for her really mean?

"I want all the actors to try out the set," Jeneva called. "Take your entrances and exits. Climb the stairs. See what parts of the set move when you shove them."

The actors wandered, vaulting over the rocks or sitting on them, leaning all their weight on the trees, finding the best way to go in and out through the netting. Some technicians moved the rocks off and then on again. Jeneva ran lightly onto the stage in her long white caftan, making minute adjustments to the branches of the maple tree. Chuck met her there, carrying a very real looking strangled rabbit that the First Witch was supposed to be tearing at in Scene One. "You want this one, or are we sticking with the rehearsal bunny?" he asked her.

"That one," Jeneva said. "It's the real thing from now on. Props have sent everything up, haven't they?"

Chuck nodded. "All but the fragile stuff. The mirror in the Apparitions Scene; a few other things. You know what Jim is like. Always worrying that things won't last the run."

"Everett," Jeneva called, "tell Props we want that mirror, and anything else they've held back."

He rumbled into his headset. Kinny strained to hear, but caught only the last bit. "...to the stage right tunnel. Thanks." He mouthed at Jeneva, "Fixed."

"Lotta props in this play," Chuck said to Jeneva.

"You can manage them, can't you?"

"Could use somebody to supervise understage."

"We'll work on it."

Kinny moved to her prompter's chair, third row center. The actors were standing in groups, chatting together or running their lines. Jeneva was on the move, speaking to Ingrid, to Everett, to the sound designer. Kinny was watching when she disappeared down the stage right tunnel that went below the audience. Lucas was watching, too. Kinny thought he looked anxious. He hovered near the tunnel, now and then looking at his watch. Jeneva was gone a long time, at least twenty minutes. When she came back her face was sweating, though it was almost too cool in the rest of the theatre. Kinny wondered what she had been doing.

"Let's go, Everett," Jeneva said tersely, returning to her seat.

"Ladies and gentlemen," Everett said, "we're going to have a fairly ordinary run-through now. You'll see a few lights and hear some sound cues, but don't feel you have to fit yourselves into them. This is your rehearsal, not a tech. If you come on in a blackout, we've glow-taped everything, but don't forget to give yourself time for your night vision to kick in. Now places please, places for the top of Act One."

Kinny opened her script and got the flashlight ready for when the house lights would go out. Everett's voice murmured into his headset. The stage lights went out, and the house lights dimmed. People stopped talking. "House out — go."

The house, the stage, everything was in blackness. "Sound Cue 3 — go." Music, weird, jangling, again with that unidentifiable familiarity. "Actors — go." Someone stumbled in the blackness; Kinny heard a muffled curse. She strained her eyes but could see nothing. Her heart thumped. The whole theatre seemed to be crackling with energy.

"Stand by Light Cue 5 and Sound Cue 4. Light Cue 5 and Sound Cue 4 — go."

Thunder crashed. Lightning flared white brilliance across the stage. Three witches in jeans and sweatsuits unwound themselves from a tightly coiled embrace.

"When shall we three meet again?" Dana Sloe, First Witch, hands full of dead rabbit, voice menacing.

The first on-stage rehearsal of Jeneva Strachan's *Macbeth* had begun.

❖ ❖ ❖

THEY PLAYED THE MUSIC AGAIN in the blackout after intermission. Kinny was certain she knew it. She tried to hum with the melody, but gave up, disturbed by the dissonance and broken rhythm. The Apparitions Scene was coming up, with Macbeth's visit to the witches, the spell that summoned the eight spectral kings, and the mirror.

Thunderclaps echoed in the blackout.

Lightning erupted blue-white over the witches' cave. A sickly violet light lingered. Now the witches could be seen, hunched and evil, moving in a circle about a cauldron that seemed to be really boiling. Smoke curled from under it in fetid ribbons, and the contents burped, thick and revolting.

In spite of herself, Kinny was fascinated. She was distracted momentarily when Macbeth entered, because the music came on again, unnatural, spiteful. *Je me souviens....* Unbidden, the French words came into Kinny's mind. *I remember.* Quebec cars had *"je me souviens"* printed on their license plates to remind French-Canadians of what they had been before 1759, when the battle on the Plains of Abraham had made Quebec a possession of the English.

The apparitions made their gory entrances from the tunnel at Kinny's left, then one after the other the eight kings. The third was Lucas; she saw him, but it was the last king in line she waited for. She hadn't seen the mirror since that day in Props when she had made something happen just by wishing for it. The eighth king came on. He held the mirror with the glass away from the audience and toward Macbeth. Alex didn't seem any different looking into it and giving his speech than he had been with the rehearsal prop in the hall downstairs. The mirror didn't seem to be affecting the eighth king either. And it hadn't bothered Jean, Kinny remembered, or Jim. What was it about her and Lucas that made them see things in it?

Macbeth finished his speech; the kings and Banquo and the witches vanished; the Scottish lord Lennox came on.

"Stop!" Jeneva called. "What's up?" Everett asked, pressing his stop watch. They had been trying to run the show without interruptions.

Jeneva hurried onstage. "I've had an idea about the witches. Can you get them back here, Everett?"

"Miss Sloe, Miss Park, Miss Gale, onstage please."

Jeneva was humming to herself. The tune was simple, so simple that at first Kinny didn't realize what she was hearing. Then her eyes widened. It was the song from the blackout, but with all the discord and tempo shifts removed. Kinny knew it now. It was an old Quebec folk song, very poignant, about a French-Canadian who feels he has lost his country. *Un Canadien Errant,* the song was called. The man sits weeping by a river and sings to it to tell his unfortunate countrymen he remembers what they have been.

Si tu vois mon pays
Mon pays malheureux
Va, dis a mes amis
Que je me souviens d'eux.

"Je me souviens," Kinny whispered, nodding slowly to herself.

The three witches were back onstage. "Picture this," Jeneva told them. "The Thane has killed Banquo to stop him from founding a royal line. Now he's seen in the mirror that Banquo's founded it anyway, through Fleance. He's sick at heart. You witches rub it in. You dance — sadistic stuff, orgiastic, plenty of Satanic overtones — all the while you're croaking out this song."

She sang it, in French. It sounded perfectly lovely. Kinny tried to imagine the witches singing it, 'croaking out' this moving and patriotic song as some vile kind of taunt. She felt as if she were choking. She had friends in Quebec, French friends. They would never understand her keeping quiet for this. She stood up. Her hands were pressed to her thighs, her breath coming in short, hard bursts. She didn't know what she was going to do, but she had to do something.

She didn't have a chance. Gwen Park said, "Jeneva, that song's almost an anthem to French-Canadians. I was in Montreal in the sixties when the students were active. I bet I heard it a dozen times a —"

"I grew up in Quebec, Gwen. I know what the song means to the French."

Gwen stood her ground. "People from

Quebec come here to see plays. Some of them are French-Canadian. To throw this song at them like that...."

"The whole play is throwing stuff at them," Jeneva replied calmly.

"But this —"

"It's just an idea, Gwen. If it doesn't work, we won't do it."

"But —"

"It's my job to have ideas," Jeneva said, suddenly steely. "It's yours to try them out. If you *want* a job, that is."

Gwen shut up. A queer silence descended over the theatre. Everett broke it. "What about taking a break, Jeneva? Since we're already stopped."

Jeneva nodded, smiled graciously at Gwen, and went off with Everett and the Musical Director. The stage emptied very quickly, actors and stage management and technicians keeping to their own separate groups. No one said anything. No one looked happy.

Kinny didn't move. She was still standing with her palms glued to her body. Whatever Jeneva said about that song being just an idea, she was going to do it. It was like that stupid toad she'd made Dana kiss on both cheeks before throwing it into the pot. Jeneva was out to get the French. She didn't care about the integrity of the play, she didn't care about the actors, she didn't care about anything except going for French Quebec's jugular.

It could be stopped. It could be stopped very easily. Kinny herself could stop it. All she had to do was go to the mirror. Kinny stood there, thinking. She was sixteen. She knew nothing about the theatre, she knew that now. Jeneva was a famous actor and director. Stratford had hired her to do this particular production her particular way. Was Kinny right to try to stop it?

But was Jeneva right to use a great play and a great theatre to make fun of one of the things an entire people held most dear?

No. No, she wasn't right.

What is owed must be paid.

All right, Dana, so if there is a price for wishing, I owe it already, don't I? Four separate wishes the first time, and a fifth later on. What's one more? Especially if I use it to help a lot of other people?

Help has its price. Power has its price. Something, or somebody, always has to pay.

But nobody else can stop Jeneva from doing this. If she's wrong, and she *is* wrong, then she has to be stopped. And if nobody can stop her but me, then I have to.

Kinny marched along the row until she came to the aisle, turned down toward the stage, and turned again, sharply, into the stage right tunnel. In the empty red-light dimness of the understage area was a table holding props from the preceding scene. The bloody doll, the sapling carried by the girl with the kneepads, the macabre head. Where was the mirror? Here, face down. Kinny reached out for it. She turned it over.

Her own face was in the glass, strange again, beautiful. She stared at it.

You will be Maiden. You will have my power.

She didn't want power. But she had French-Canadian friends who trusted her. She had people she'd stood up for in the past. Could she look them in the face again if she didn't do what she could here to help? Could she look herself in the face? Responsibility wasn't the same thing as power. She had to do it.

"Don't let Jeneva do it," Kinny said aloud to the face in the mirror, and then, to make it very clear, "I wish that Jeneva will decide not to use the song that way."

Kinny held her breath. Nothing happened. She blinked. When she looked again her image was ordinary, no longer flower-decked and beautiful. Sighing, she put down the mirror. She had been angry, but now she was just tired, tired and afraid.

She'd made a wish on the mirror. She done it willfully, when for more than a week she'd been determined never even to look in the mirror again. Five wishes, now six. Where would it end?

Today, she thought. It must end today.

After the break Jeneva swept onto the stage where the three witches were waiting, gave a forgiving hug to Gwen, and said, "I've rethought. We're running long, this act. Let's stick to our original format."

"We're not going to do that song?" Gwen asked, blinking at her.

Jeneva shook her head, smiling tightly. "We don't want to be too obvious."

There was a murmur of relief from the rest of the cast, a visible release of tension. I should be happy, Kinny told herself dully. But an old proverb was running in her mind, over and over, endlessly.

"Be careful what you wish for. You may get it."

Chapter Twelve

T HE PHOTOGRAPHER STOOD HALFWAY UP A ladder just below the bottom step of the stage. "Too many shadows," he called over his shoulder. The light on stage increased. The man peered through his lens again.

Arms round each other, black-gaitered legs straining passionately against skirted ones, Alex and Meredith were staring soulfully into each other's eyes, trying to maintain the pose for the photographer while telling each other jokes. Lady Macbeth's letter lay on the floor beside them. Suddenly Meredith laughed aloud.

"Hey, you two, sex please, not fun and games," Jeneva reminded them sharply.

"Sorry, darling," Meredith said, and became Lady Macbeth once more, greeting her husband, the new Thane of Cawdor home from the war and ready to murder Duncan. The photographer snapped madly away. "Thank you," Everett called. "Next scene, please. Duncan and retinue being welcomed by Lady M."

The scene changed — sunset into night; oil-lamps and curling mist. Chuck picked up Lady Macbeth's letter and took it backstage. Lucas watched restlessly from the wings. His eyes burned with fatigue. These days he was hardly sleeping at all. Sometimes, rarely, he would drop like a stone into bed and instantly be asleep, but almost always he'd wake an hour later in a panic, imagining that someone was standing in the corner of his room, watching him. Heart thudding, he would flick on the light. There was never anyone there. Other nights he would lie awake hour after hour, making himself stay there when all he wanted to do was jump out of bed in the dark and go over to the window and peer out. Sometimes he let himself do it, straining for minutes on end to see something through the dirty glass while words echoed in his brain.

"She knows about the boy?"

"He's part of it."

He could never be sure if he actually saw anything. But now and then he conjured up a humped shape in the dark shadows of a tree. He knew it was probably his imagination, but that didn't seem to help.

He had never liked his room, but now he found himself avoiding it, spending his free hours at the library or the Y and coming home only when everything else was closed. He wore the medallion all the time, even in the shower, though he had to dry it carefully afterward, to prevent rust. He could feel it against his skin now, far down under his layers of costume. It pleased him to be wearing a Celtic symbol, something similar to what people wore in the real Macbeth's period, under all the foolishness of this French costume.

He'd always pictured Fleance as a youngish boy in a travel-stained cloak and tartan breeches, or possibly a kilt – a simple squire for his noble Scottish father Banquo. But Jeneva wanted Fleance to be identifiably French and more strongly linked to the military power in Quebec, and so he was wearing the garb of a drummer of the Royal Roussillon Regiment. Blue coat and red waistcoat edged with royal lace, silver grey breeches, white gaiters, round-toed black shoes, even a hat, black with gold trim. Lucas could only be grateful Fleance was young enough not to need aristocratic makeup or a wig.

Photo shoots were boring for actors. You came out in full costume and took up your position and tried to feel the character inside you while a photographer poked his camera in your face and technicians came and went at your back. Tech week was full of things like this – cue-to-cue rehearsals where all you acted was the bit of a scene where a sound or light cue changed; dreary periods of waiting while the chief carpenter mused over some bit of set noise the designer hated; exit lines repeated over and over again for the stage manager, who wanted three seconds pared from a scene change and was willing to spend an hour to make sure it happened. Once a day, maybe, you actually acted – four hours at most out of ten, or even twelve. It was a wearisome, unreal time, knowing that all the technical details had to be ironed out in this last week before the paying audiences arrived, but feeling somehow that what was really important, the actual play, had been shoved aside as secondary.

"Hi, Lucas. Hot costume." It was Kinny, carrying a powdered, jeweled wig.

"More than you know," he said, putting his finger down his collar to let out billows of imaginary steam.

They both stood there, awkwardly. Neither could think of anything else to say. The mirror came between them. Their feelings about it were just not the same.

Lucas knew she disapproved of his going to it so often, that she even pitied him for wanting to look into it. Well, he pitied her too. She would never get close to the real Macbeth. She would never feel what it was like to face the choices of the last great Scottish king. She would never know what really had happened in 1057. She was passing up on a great opportunity, and he was glad of it because that made the real Macbeth his alone.

But it made it harder, too. He was the only person in Stratford who knew the truth, the only person for whom Jeneva's production was revealed as the utter travesty of justice that it was. His outrage grew daily, but there was nothing he could do. He couldn't even talk about it. No one would believe him, not even Kinny, who was too scared of the mirror to believe it could contain so much good.

Sometimes when the mirror was being used on stage and he looked at Kinny he thought she wasn't just scared of it. She was resisting the compulsion to go near the mirror, but Lucas was sure she felt it all the same. It was as if there was something private going on between her and the mirror, something that had nothing to do with him. Lucas didn't understand that at all, and he liked it less.

These days the mirror was being stored with all the other props in the busy backstage area. Lucas spent a lot of each day hovering backstage, waiting for opportunities to look into the mirror unobserved. It wasn't easy. The crew always seemed to be around, or the assistant stage managers would be going up and down the rows checking the Props. Sometimes it was Jeneva who was inspecting them. Jeneva was spending a lot more time backstage than Lucas wanted. He wished she'd get out front where she belonged.

Sometimes, not often, it worried him a little

that he spent so much time thinking about the mirror. But more and more it was only the mirror that made it bearable for him to stay in Stratford at all. What he had seen in the mirror got him through the sleepless nights, because if Macbeth had survived a darkness like the one Lucas had witnessed him suffer, then who was Lucas to let some reasonless and inexplicable fear get him down? It got him through rehearsals too, because it was a spark of truth to cling to in all the falseness. That was a mixed blessing, because it emphasized the falseness as well. He pictured Alex Blair wearing the foppish wig Kinny was carrying, and remembered the real Macbeth with his dark hair flowing free under a simple gold diadem, and he was angry suddenly, angry as he was so often these days, and with no possible outlet.

"It's for the Banquet Scene," Kinny said, seeing him frowning at the wig in her hand.

"You back working for Props?" Lucas asked, for something to say.

"For anybody who needs me," she replied. "I'll be out of a prompting job once the show opens. But Jeneva says I can help supervise with props. Understage, probably...."

Without at all knowing he was going to do it, he said savagely, "I'd like to cut up that wig."

She turned her green eyes full on his face. "You wouldn't wear it if it was you playing the

Thane. You'd tell Jeneva you wouldn't."

"I'm too young to play Mac – the Thane. I could understudy him, but Norris is already doing that."

"Would it be...satisfying, understudying? I mean, if you really wanted to play a particular role?"

"At least an understudy could rehearse it decently," he said bitterly, "which is a heck of a lot better than what Alex is doing now. Everett runs understudy rehearsals, see, not Jeneva. He's a stickler for where to stand and what to do and when to do it, but as long as you use the right words he doesn't give a damn how you say them. Not like Jeneva and her Marquis de Sade crap. Norris could rehearse it reasonably, if he wanted. He'd never get it right. The *play's* not right. But he could at least –"

He broke off. He was suddenly aware of the Celtic medallion. It felt hot. It hadn't felt hot like this since that night on the island. He rubbed his chest nervously, his eyes hunting the shadows. Was someone over there in the dimly lit area by the assistant stage manager's booth? He strained his eyes. No. But farther back, near the Props Storage area, that hunched shape.... Was it real, or not? The last time the hunchbacked woman had come into the theatre had been when the mirror arrived in the rehearsal hall. He rubbed his thumb over the white burn scar on his right palm. And the time before that had been when Joan Mackenzie.... Was that shape moving? He squinted after it. Yes. It was definitely heading into the Props Storage area. The place where the mirror was.

He strode forward, urgency propelling him. He almost didn't notice Kinny grabbing his arm. "You're going to that mirror again, aren't you?" she demanded, dragging at him so that he had to listen.

"Let go," he said.

"Don't, Lucas. You're obsessed with that mirror. It's not safe for you. Please don't −"

"Let go!"

"Lucas, please, I have to know something." Her hand still gripped him tightly. "Is the reason you keep going to the mirror because you wish into it?"

He was angry now, so angry that he began prying at Kinny's fingers. "What is this, 'Snow White'? Mirror mirror on the wall, please let Jeneva take a fall. You really must think I'm out of my −"

"Stop," Kinny whispered. "You're hurting my hand. Stop." Her eyes, huge with misery, stared at him. Under his prying, scratching fingers, her hand felt small and helpless, like a bird he'd injured.

Ashamed, he took his hand away. She stepped back from him, dropping her arm to her side. The hunched shape was out of sight now. There was no time to be lost. "I've got to go," Lucas said.

She gave him an empty, dreary look. "I guess I have to help you," she said. "It's my fault, anyway. You'd never have even seen that mirror if I —"

He was in too much of a hurry to listen. He sped toward the Props area, practically knocking over Dana Sloe, who was coming off stage. She was in costume — a filthy peasant skirt and torn shawl. Her wig appeared to have bits of raw meat stuck in it. "Don't miss your entrance, Lucas," she said, smiling horrifyingly through her witch's makeup.

Lucas blinked, then whirled to see what was happening onstage. Dana was right. They'd called his scene. Banquo was already on. He had no choice. As he set himself at Banquo's side he saw Kinny disappearing toward the backstage Prop Storage area. Maybe she'd seen the hunchback too, and was going to investigate.

"I guess I have to help you," she had said. And, "Is the reason you keep going to the mirror because you wish into it?" What had she meant by that?

"The photographer's waiting, Lucas," Everett announced meaningly.

Lucas shook himself. Fleance, he said to himself, I'm Fleance. Banquo gave him his cue.

He said his two lines. The photographer took his shots. Jeneva made a suggestion. They changed position. More shots. It was twenty minutes before he could get away. When he finally got to the backstage storage area, he found it deserted, but to his relief, the mirror was still there. He began to pick it up, then stopped, frowning. He'd left it face down the last time he'd looked in it, only an hour or so before. It hadn't been used on stage since then. But now the blue glass was gleaming palely at him in the dim backstage light.

In the last hour, someone had been handling it.

🏵 🏵 🏵

IN STREET CLOTHES AT LAST, Lucas sat in his favourite spot in the audience, four rows back from the stage manager's table, anonymous in the dimly lit house but still close enough to see the expressions on the actors' faces. It was almost six o'clock and the photo shoot was drawing to a close. He could have gone early for dinner, or to the Y for a workout, but he stayed. Onstage they were doing the dramatic sword fight between Macduff and Macbeth.

Fight sequences were dangerous on any set. On this one, with the shrubs and rocks of the Plains of Abraham littering the foreground and the palisaded city wall closing off the area under the balcony, the amount of open space was perilously small. There was a superb fencing master at Stratford who not only taught the actors but also choreographed every single move the fighters made. It was like a ballet or a military drill, everything done slowly at first and with loud counting — and ONE, a lift of the sword, and TWO, hold while your opponent leaps sideways, and THREE, thrust, and FOUR, step back and parry. Over and over again in one of the small rehearsal halls, just you and your opponent and the fight master and his drum. Hundreds of moves to memorize and perform in order, and when it was time, on the set, where they were done faster and faster until the adrenalin surged and the thing became, for the actors as well as for anyone watching, something that went beyond pretense. It was then that things got really dangerous. The swords were perfect replicas of eighteenth century soldiers' sabers, and they were sharp and strong and there were no safety tips on the ends. Lucas knew an actor in Chicago who'd lost half a tooth and part of a forearm in a sword fight on stage; he had heard of others who'd lost eyes, ears, and even their lives.

But this was only a photo shoot. They were taking the fight scene desultorily, the photographer calling halts as he moved in and out of sword range. Jon Crowell still had some spring in his step, but Alex looked tired and worn.

Disillusioned, almost, Lucas thought. Briefly, he wondered what kind of Macbeth Alex would have made, if things had been different.

"You've got to turn savage here, Alex," Jeneva called. She was sitting in the same row as Lucas, some distance away. She stood up. "You've killed Macduff's wife and children, and you know he'll kill you if he can. You're a cornered rat. Let's see it."

Alex signaled that he understood. He threw his shoulders back and bared his teeth at Jon while swinging his sword. Jon's great saber rang against his. Again. "Good," Jeneva murmured. "Good." The photographer snapped madly away. Sparks flew; again iron clanged against iron. It was the very sound Lucas always imagined when he tried to reconstruct the scene that led Macbeth to make his plea to the witches. Great Scottish claymores battering one another in Lumphanan Bottom, Macbeth's forces taking the worst of it, red blood in the river and....

His chest hurt. Lucas stiffened in his seat. It was the medallion. It felt as if it were on fire. He clutched it, staring wildly around. The hunchback was near. He was sure of it. Where? Just at the edge of the stage, there was something – what was it? – something in the wings. A flicker of movement that shouldn't have been there, doing something.... What?

Then it happened. He didn't see it. He was

too busy looking stage right, but he heard it. A kind of a whoosh at stage left, then a dull thud and an odd skittering noise, followed by a frightened "Alex!" in Jon Crowell's voice. Jeneva had hoisted up her caftan and was running for the stage, trailing a thin, teakettle shriek behind her. At stage left, there was a prone man dressed in a waistcoat and strangely red collar ruffles. Jon Crowell in British scarlet bent over him, but the scarlet was dripping its colour onto the floor....

Lucas got slowly to his feet. Waves of dizziness assailed him. Pandemonium. A person couldn't think when there was this much noise. He put his hands to his ears. His eyes wouldn't focus; there was something in them, something stinging and blurry. He wanted to rub them, but if he took his hands off his ears he'd hear things again, and he didn't want to, he'd heard too much already, he didn't want to hear any more. He blinked; something rolled down his cheek; he could see again, if he didn't let himself look at too much all at once. He wanted to see only one thing, anyway. There were people in the way. He stood up on his seat to get higher, and looked.

It was Alex on the floor. Lucas hadn't been sure before, because the head hadn't been quite...right. He looked at it very carefully now, analyzing. Yes. Too much to the side

And then...that red stuff.

Someone was holding on to him, arms around his legs. "Let go," he said calmly. "I want to see."

"Lucas! Lucas!" He heard that even though he'd blocked his ears.

"Go away."

The arms struck at him, hands clawing at his legs. It hurt. He frowned. He looked down. Slowly his arms fell to his side. He got down off his seat.

"Kinny?"

She was panting in tiny shallow gasps, her lips blue. Her pupils were small as pinpricks. Her words came out in telegraphic little bundles. "...didn't mean...but if it's my fault...if I...oh, if it was because I...."

Her terror was invading him. His knees went weak. He sat down, pulling her on top of him. But her babbling didn't stop. "You wouldn't ever have seen the mirror if I hadn't...so I thought, if you got some of what you wanted you might not...so I wished...if Norris could get a better role then you could, but I didn't mean that role. NOT THAT ROLE!" It ended in a wail that chilled his blood.

"Shh. Shh." He pulled her face roughly into his chest, forcing her to silence. He didn't know what else to do. She shuddered against him. "Listen to me," he said, very calmly, very quietly.

"Alex has had an accident. It happens, sometimes, in sword fights. He is...hurt...."

"Excuse me," Everett Lunn said courteously from the row in front of them. "I see that you're busy, but if you wouldn't mind just having a look under your seat? I seem to have lost my pocket notebook, and it's got my doctor's phone number in it. There's a bit of a rush, so...."

Over Kinny's head Lucas stared at him in horror. The little red notebook was where it always was, sticking out of Everett's shirt pocket. "You want — a doctor?" Lucas got out at last.

"For Alex," Everett said wisely.

Lucas stared at him helplessly, mechanically patting Kinny's jerking back. Onstage, Jeneva was shouting Everett's name with all the projection of her actor's lungs. He never even looked at her. After a moment he backed off down the row of seats, peering now and then at the floor.

And then, suddenly, Dana Sloe was standing beside Lucas, but she was addressing Kinny, still shuddering in Lucas's arms. "You shouldn't grieve so."

Kinny shook off Lucas' restraining hands and turned swollen eyes to Dana's face. "What if it's...? Maybe it's my fault!"

"Things of power." Dana said, suddenly

stern. "I did warn you. You knew."

Lucas flared at her, "Shut up, will you? Can't you see?"

"This is between the child and myself."

"No, Dana," Kinny said. Her face was ravaged, not at all young or pretty. "He's got to understand." She turned to him. "I wished, Lucas. It was for you. It was so you wouldn't keep going to the mirror."

"I don't know what you're talking about." He didn't want to hear. He didn't want to know.

"Listen, you've got to understand so you won't...I have to say it right...LISTEN!" She took a huge breath. "You were a slave to that mirror. It was bad for you. Dangerous. You needed something else to think about. And I knew you wanted to understudy the Thane —"

"Macbeth," Lucas said through his teeth, "Macbeth, not *the Thane.*"

"— and I thought, if you did, the mirror wouldn't matter so much to you any more. So I made a wish —"

Mirror, mirror on the wall....

"— and now Alex is —"

Lucas stared at her in horror.

"— and that means Norris will be playing the Thane, don't you see? I wished he'd get a better...." She gulped, her eyes wide and horrified.

Dana said, "You wished Norris would get a

better role, so that Lucas could take his place as Alex's understudy."

Lucas wanted to scream. "What are you two talking about? What do you *mean?*"

"If you'd listen you'd know!" Kinny shouted at him. "I wanted to get you a chance to understudy Macbeth! To get you away from that mirror! Don't you see? And now —"

"You don't seriously think this play is going to continue with its lead player dead, do you?"

She gave a single harsh sob. "I...oh, Lucas, do you really think it won't? Because then when Norris gets a better role it won't be that one. I won't have — it won't be my wish that caused...." She sobbed again.

The enormity of what she was saying washed over Lucas. He put his head in his hands. "Wishes don't cause people to die," he muttered wretchedly. "I don't believe it. I won't." Through his misery he was aware that Kinny was in Dana's arms, and that Dana was comforting her in a soft, private, almost singsong voice that he didn't want to listen to. But he couldn't stop himself from hearing.

"Ah, child," she said, "I would take this pain from you if I could, but you let it in, it is yours. A wish, an opening, and Power rushes in. It is a wind from the north, it will do its damage. The choice is not yours, though you began it. You cannot even control it, not as you are. You must change first, for that kind of control; you must learn."

Lucas lifted his head. "She wants something from you, Kinny," he said. He didn't intend to say it. He didn't even know what he meant by it. And Dana was right there, listening. "Stay away from her," he added hoarsely, and he intended it for Kinny, but somehow he knew it applied just as much to himself.

Dana dropped her arms from Kinny's body. She turned her eyes to his. Lucas felt a pain in his chest, almost a burning. "What you know fills less than a page," she said, like someone passing judgment. "This play will go on, whatever you say, and the part you play in it will not be an easy one."

"I don't...what do you...?"

But Dana had walked away.

"What did she mean, Kinny?"

"You're going to understudy Macbeth." Drearily.

"They'll never ask me. Even if Norris does get the lead —"

"They will ask you. Who else has been to every rehearsal? Who else knows the part by heart?"

"I wouldn't take the part." But he knew he would.

"It was to keep you away from the mirror. I thought if you got to play Macbeth —"

He laughed suddenly, bitterly, harshly.

"What's the matter, Lucas? What do you mean?"

He stopped laughing as suddenly as he'd begun. "You think if I play Macbeth it'll keep my mind off the mirror? It won't. It can't. Because it's Macbeth who is in that mirror! It's Macbeth I go to the mirror to see!"

SCOTLAND

Chapter Thirteen

I N THE BRIGHT SUMMER SUNLIGHT, COOLER and sharper-edged than in Canada, Edinburgh seemed a busy, modern place, full of tourists and theatre people here for the opening of the Festival. In reality it was an old, old city, a place fortified for fifteen centuries against bloody conquest. Sometimes it had defeated its invaders and sometimes, as with Henry VIII, it merely outlasted them. It had contributed its own share of horror over the years – executions of heroes like Montrose, the martyrdom of more than a hundred Covenanters, daily witch burnings at the Castle. For centuries, off and on, human agony had risen like clouds of smoke over the city. Like smoke too, none of it had lasted.

Kinny knew that many of the things that had happened here had been even more appalling than the death of Alexander Blair, yet clearly the human spirit had survived it all. Descendants of people who had died violent and horrible deaths now greeted other people cheerily in the streets, or hurried to ordinary jobs selling shoes or baking scones or putting on plays. There was something reassuring about that to Kinny, who had arrived a week ago, thinner than she had ever been and wondering if she would ever sleep without nightmares again.

She was walking with Lucas down the street known as the Royal Mile. Twentieth century street-paving lay side by side with five-hundred-year-old cobblestones, but there was so much litter it was hard to tell where one stopped and the other began. Posters and flyers for the Edinburgh Festival littered the streets, along with candy wrappers, cigarette butts, old newspapers and puddles of abandoned ice cream. You couldn't walk without stepping on something. All around was the reek of fish-and-chips and malt vinegar and ancient mould and sweat. There were other sights and smells, no more regal, despite the towering bulk of the Castle behind them to the west and Holyrood Palace less than a mile ahead.

"I don't know why they call it the Royal Mile," Kinny said. "It doesn't seem at all regal."

"It doesn't, does it?" Lucas replied. "Royal robes would need laundering after about three steps here."

She and Lucas were spending a lot of time together here in Scotland, as they had ever since Alex's death. It was an odd, uncomfortable togetherness. Neither of them got any noticeable pleasure out of it. Lucas maintained the same inscrutable politeness with Kinny that he did with everyone else. The only difference was that he made an effort to be with her.

She seldom ever knew what he was thinking. They spoke rarely, and only about the weather or a performance or something that didn't matter at all to either of them. In those first horrible days after Alex's death they had discussed the mirror and discussed it until neither of them could bear it any more. They simply couldn't agree. She knew — she *knew* — that the mirror was evil and dangerous, and not only to her. He argued that the mirror had never offered him any wishes, that what he saw was history, a few moments in the life of the real Macbeth, and that history could not harm him. She hadn't gone near the mirror since the day of Alex's death, but she knew that Lucas often did. The mirror was like a high wall between them, preventing understanding or even real friendship. Yet whenever Kinny was by herself at the theatre, and especially when Dana Sloe came near her, she would look up to find Lucas coming her way.

Kinny didn't know how he felt about his new role as Macbeth's understudy. That was one of the things they couldn't discuss. She had wished him the role, and a man had died to get it for him. A man had died. Even now, five weeks after it had happened, the thought could make her so sick she had to curl up on the bathroom floor with her head pressed against the base of the toilet, waiting for the sickness to subside. Because of her disastrous wish on the mirror, because she had had the arrogance to think she knew what was best for Lucas and how she might get it for him, a man had died. And it hadn't been best for Lucas. It hadn't distracted him from looking in the mirror. If anything he went to it even more than he had before. Her wish had backfired, and it had killed a man.

Sometimes she wondered how she could bear Lucas' presence at all. But she needed it; she needed someone with her who knew the truth of what had happened. Only Dana and Lucas could know that, and of the two, only Lucas didn't want something from her. It made him comforting to be with, even when they had nothing to give one another but reminders of the terrible days in Stratford, and silence.

She had dragged herself through the last four weeks at Stratford on almost no sleep. She had nightmares every night, red ones, terrifying. In them she was always aware of a Power waiting somewhere for her to make a mistake, a Power that might come to her without her knowing it, and then would refuse to be limited by her. She would wake, trembling and choking, and in her mind would hear Dana's words about openings and winds from the north and having to change and learn. And then all day those same words would sit in her stomach like something cold and indigestible, a responsibility she hadn't fulfilled.

She would go to the theatre three hours early, skipping breakfast so she wouldn't have to see Dana. The only way to avoid the crowds of ghouls who waited by the stage door for a glimpse of someone belonging to the infamous *Macbeth* company was to slip through the business office. Once in the Green Room she would drink pots and pots of tea while the actors whispered around her like flies buzzing. Dana came in nearly every time Kinny was there, and very often the only empty seat would be at Kinny's side. She would pull out the chair, smile at Kinny, and sit, stirring rings in her tea until it was almost cold. She never said much. Invariably, as the minutes went by and Dana's teaspoon clinked and clinked, Kinny would find that all she could think about was that the mirror was not done with her. However much she might avoid it, the mirror had given her what she asked for, and something was now expected of her in return. It was only a matter of time. And Dana would sit there stirring her tea while the silence grew until Kinny knew she was going to have to break it no matter what, and then somebody – usually Lucas – would come in and the stirring would stop and Dana would be gone. Other people came and went — Jeneva like a white-faced storm-trooper; Everett clumping in with his red notebook in one hand and a Danish in the other, getting fatter and louder every day. Nobody connected with the *Macbeth* production was happy.

It had been Jon Crowell's hand that had dealt Alex's death blow, and even though the inquest had found the death to be an accident and declared specifically that Jon was totally blameless, he had left Stratford a few days later. People said he was quitting acting for good. The fight master had stepped into Jon's role as Macduff, and he and Norris had spent many long hours rehearsing the terrible fight that caused Macbeth's death. Rumours abounded. People said Norris had asked for danger pay to play Macbeth. Some said Jeneva had told Everett that if there had been even one more week before opening she would have tried to get somebody else. But when it came to the actual production, there was no back-biting. Everyone had tried hard to help the new Macbeth and Macduff, no matter how many extra rehearsals were called. Kinny learned for the first time how important was the old theatre tradition that "the show must go on." No one other than Jon had threatened to leave. They were a company under siege, and the siege mentality united them.

It had become impossible to go anywhere in Stratford without someone asking them for their firsthand views about what had happened and how it had felt and didn't they want to leave the production and weren't they afraid. Lucas, Dana and Norris had been bothered more than anyone; Lucas because someone had dug up the story about his burned hand, and the other two because they had had to take over from Joan and Alex. Everywhere they went they had been hounded by occultists and thrill-seekers and interview-hungry reporters, asking them what it felt like to be on intimate terms with a curse.

Less than a week after Alex died, *Macbeth* had had its opening. It had been a wretched night. Norris had played Macbeth like a lisping combination of Al Capone and Louis XIV, and there had been little choice for the rest of the cast but to respond in kind. The result had been a performance where the anti-French statement was everything. The critics had hated it, lavishly and at length. In Ottawa there had been big demonstrations against bigotry in the arts. Quebec sovereigntists – the new name for those who wanted Quebec to separate from the rest of Canada – had had a field day. Stratford's *Macbeth* had made the papers all across the country. People phoned their Members of Parliament, complaining that this nationally-

funded theatre now threatened the nation's continued existence. Jeneva might have been pleased at the extent to which her views had reached the whole country except that the very next day she had been summoned to an emergency meeting with Stratford's Board of Governors.

No one knew exactly what had happened at that meeting. But when she'd come out of it, grim-faced with fury, an emergency rehearsal had been called for the entire *Macbeth* company. Norris was to drop the lisp, she had announced crisply. They were to remember that this was Shakespeare, and not just Canadian politics. She'd said this last sentence as if it were a line she'd been forced to memorize.

From then on there had been extra rehearsals every day. Norris had become less glaringly depraved, and there were one or two cautious improvements from the rest of the cast. It had satisfied the Board, but Jeneva obviously hated it. The hardest thing to endure had been the audiences. They had come to *Macbeth* in droves, but they didn't come for the play; they came to see if the curse would kill anyone else in front of their eyes.

Scotland was a new chance for everyone. So far nobody in Edinburgh seemed to know about the disasters this *Macbeth* had undergone in Canada. They were opening tonight in

one of the auditorium doors. Kinny didn't know why, but she felt nervous. She put out a hand, not quite touching Lucas' sleeve. But he was forging ahead and didn't notice. She followed, her heart beating uncomfortably hard.

Inside the auditorium, lamp check was going on. One after another the individual stage lamps were being tested, with an electrician in the high control booth switching them on and off as a technician onstage called out each lamp's number and "okay" after the lamp lit satisfactorily. There were no other lights on in the house. Between lamps Kinny couldn't even see Lucas as he walked ahead of her down the aisle. The air felt hot, stifling almost. It had an odd, chemical smell to it.

"Twenty-three, okay," the technician called. He moved. The lamp went out. In the darkness before the next lamp went on, Kinny was sure something moved in the row of benches to her left. A circle of dim light went on onstage. Kinny blinked to her left. Nothing. But there had been something —

"Twenty-four, okay." Again, darkness. This time Kinny was sure. There was a stink like gasoline, and someone brushed by her, half spinning her around. "Hey!" she said angrily.

"What's up, Kinny?" came Lucas' voice.

"Where's twenty-five?" the technician called from the darkened stage. "Got some trouble up there with twenty-five?"

"Lucas, there's someone here. I smelled –"

"Who's smoking in here?" someone yelled from backstage. "Don't you know this place is a firetrap? All the signs we've posted, can't you read?"

There was a sudden whoosh of air, a furnace-like roaring, a red-hot glare where before there had been only darkness. A blast of pressure slammed into Kinny and she fell backward; a bench toppled onto her. She felt rather than heard glass shatter. Somewhere a door slammed.

"Clear the theatre! Fire! Fire! Christ, where's the extinguisher?"

"Kinny?" Lucas' voice. "Kinny, where are you?"

Her chest hurt. Fire shadows danced on the ceiling. Someone dragged the bench off her body. Someone hauled her up. "Can you move? I can carry you."

"I'm all right."

"Then come on! Fast!"

She ran. Lucas had her hand, hauling her along the shortest way out of the auditorium, which was toward the blackout cloth that curtained off the west wing. The fire was licking the stage as they ran by. Kinny was panting, each breath squeezing her chest like a giant hot hand. Lucas let go of her to push the curtains away. There were lights behind, and people, actors in costume peering in from the hall and technicians shooing them away, someone with a megaphone, someone else with a bucket of earth. "Get out of here, you idiots!" someone bellowed. Kinny saw Lucas stumble over to the props table, paw frantically for something, grab it. She knew what it was. Sickened, she turned away.

Outside, the marbled corridor was charged with human panic. People were running in every direction, their arms full of props and other things too valuable to leave. The big wooden doors were flung open. Above the babble Kinny could hear someone on the phone shouting the fire's location.

Jeneva was the only one who wasn't running. Instead she stood with her back pressed against the beautiful carved panelling that separated the auditorium from the outside world, watching as her production fell apart before her sunken eyes. And on her white face was a look that Kinny had never seen on anyone's face, never before in all her life.

Chapter Fourteen

"**T**HE THING I'D LIKE TO KNOW IS," Christine said querulously, "how they're going to make sure nothing like that ever happens again. I mean, what would have happened if the fire had been started with the audience actually there? People could have died!"

"*We're* already dead," Adam answered her gloomily, "artistically if not otherwise. A few good reviews on this tour was our only chance to get out of the poop in Canada. But now it'll be the Scottish play's curse that will get reviewed, not our production."

Lucas sat silently over his coffee at their bed-and-breakfast. Adam was right. A bare twelve hours after the firefighters had left the auditorium of the Assembly Hall a smoking, dripping mess, all the major British newspapers had got hold of the story about the disasters Jeneva Strachan's *Macbeth* had undergone in Canada. Front page articles went into detail about Joan's electrocution, Alex's severed jugular and Lucas' burned hand; headlines screamed phrases like "Scottish Hall in flames: Macbeth the cause" or "Assembly Hall the latest curse victim?" The more important newspapers made it clear that an obscure Quebec extremist group had claimed responsibility for setting the fire, with the stated intention of drawing international attention to "government-funded Canadian bigotry." A few of the newspapers explained how Jeneva's production was a kind of allegory about the conflict between French Quebec and English Canada. But to most of Edinburgh – even to most of Britain – the thing that would be remembered about Jeneva's *Macbeth* was that it appeared to be under some kind of supernatural curse.

Lucas knew Kinny had smelled gasoline just before the explosion. He knew someone had bumped into her, escaping before the fire burst out. He knew that a French-Canadian group had claimed responsibility. It all pointed perfectly clearly to an ordinary act of political sabotage. But Lucas couldn't forget what he had seen when he and Kinny entered the auditorium while lamp check was going on. He had been ahead of Kinny, and didn't think she had noticed. But he had. In the brief moment while the number twenty-two lamp was on he had seen a dark, humped shape in the east wings.

There had been no sign of the hunchbacked woman since the day of Alex's death. Was she here in Scotland now? Was her presence connected in some way with the fire? Whenever anything bad happened in the company, the hunchback was nearby. It stretched belief to imagine it was just coincidence.

Norris came into the breakfast room wearing tennis shoes, boxer shorts, and a t-shirt. "Hey, gang, you'll never guess what Jeneva's done."

"What?" Christine and Adam said at once.

"She's got us a holiday. I jogged over to her hotel before breakfast and Chuck told me. Five days off for the whole cast while the Assembly Hall's being repaired. A morale booster, I guess. She's booked a bus tour for the duration and we're all going. Not the technicians and Everett and Chuck, but all the rest of us."

"Is Stratford paying?" Christine demanded.

"So I hear," Norris said. "They have to pay our room and board on tour anyway, and it's probably cheaper outside Edinburgh. Mmm, those scones look good."

"I'll bet Jeneva's arranged that tour so we can't talk to the media," Adam said.

"Is it only going to take five days to repair the Hall?" Lucas asked Norris.

"The damage looked worse than it was," the other replied. "Only the end of the stage and the maple tree are in really bad shape. None of the costumes or props were damaged."

Just then Kinny came in. She looked as if she hadn't slept a wink. Lucas turned to her in relief. "We're going on a bus tour," he told her.

"Where?" she asked.

"Don't know. Where, Norris?"

Norris answered through a mouthful of scone. "Thane territory."

"What?"

"You know. Our Thane. The Big Mac. Where he was born, his castles, where he died, that sort of thing."

Lucas' heart thudded. "The real Thane?" he asked. "Or Shakespeare's?"

Norris' eyebrows quirked. "What's the difference?"

"I should have known it'd be a tour like that," Adam said, groaning a little. "Dry-as-dust historical facts, gift shops full of marmalade jars, nothing to do in the evenings...Jeneva will call it research, and use it as a tax write-off. Quel bore."

"For how long?" Kinny asked, still looking at Lucas.

"Five days. Just till the Hall's ready for us again."

"Then we're definitely going to open? Jeneva's not canceling the show?"

"She's determined not to," Norris said. "There'll only be a two-week run, but two weeks at the Edinburgh Festival are better than two years in most towns. I for one am glad we're going ahead with it. I've worked like a dog to get ready for this opening. Of course, that was when there was a chance of getting a decent review." He reached gloomily for another scone.

"We've all worked hard, Norris," Christine said. "You're not the only one."

Norris ignored her. "Chuck told me Jeneva didn't get any sleep at all last night, she was so busy arranging things. She spent an hour on the phone with Canadian Actors' Equity, and about twice that with the insurance types. Right now she's hiring some security guards and talking to the owners of the Assembly Hall."

"Pretty efficient," Adam said grudgingly. "A fire like that would be the last straw for most directors, especially after everything else that's happened. I'm surprised Jeneva's dealing with it so well."

"Yes, but did you see her face last night?" Christine demanded. "I tell you, if ever somebody was mad enough to commit murder...."

"When do we leave, Norris?" Kinny asked a little hoarsely.

"This afternoon."

"Oh." Kinny hesitated. "I guess I'd better go pack."

Lucas watched her leave. She hadn't had any breakfast. And that look in her eyes....What was wrong with her? She reminded him of a rabbit frozen helplessly in the headlights of a car that was swooping down on it. She often looked like that these days. It was one of the reasons why he felt he had to protect her.

Dana Sloe was another. He had to keep her away from Kinny. He'd done as much of that as he could for the last five weeks: sitting beside Kinny at lunch whenever Dana was near, walking her home in Stratford and making sure she was locked in her bedroom before he left, quietly paying their landlady here in Edinburgh to call Kinny's room a single and so prevent Dana from trying to share it with her. Dana wasn't even staying in the same house as Kinny now. Lucas had managed that by getting Norris to take the last room. He had done everything he could think of to keep Dana and Kinny apart. And every time he succeeded, Dana looked at him with her round, glittery eyes, and the iron pendant he still wore burned against his chest.

Without at all understanding how he knew, Lucas was certain that Dana was immensely dangerous to Kinny. That final wish of Kinny's had given Dana some kind of power over her. *I did warn you*, Dana had said to her after Alex's death, and *the choice is not yours, though. You began it.* Exactly what she meant by that, Lucas didn't like to think, but it worried him. It worried him as well that Dana seemed to take it for granted that the mirror could give Kinny whatever she wished for. What did Dana know about that mirror? And how did she know it?

Lucas sipped his coffee. It was cold, but he scarcely noticed. His head ached. Too many questions, he told himself, too much thinking. That hunchbacked woman, for instance. She and Dana were allied, he had known that from the time in the rehearsal hall when they'd both concentrated so hard on Jeneva and the mirror. Right after that Jeneva had changed her earlier orders to decorate the mirror, saying she didn't want it altered in any way. Was that why Dana and the hunchback had looked at Jeneva like that? To make sure the mirror stayed the way it was for some purpose of their own? How many of the other awful things that had happened were because those two wanted – or needed – them to?

Lucas was almost sure that the time he had followed Dana to the island in Stratford it had been the hunchbacked woman she had talked to. "Did you communicate with our Sister?" the other person had asked. *Our* Sister, she had said. Which meant, if Lucas was right, that Dana and the hunchback were sisters already, and they had another one somewhere. Three sisters. Three weird sisters. The phrase jangled in his head. Where was the third, then? "She's been too long a prisoner," Dana had said. So the third sister was in prison somewhere. But she could communicate with Dana somehow, or Dana with her. "She says she has a plan." And, "She won't let us just take it and go."

Take what and go?

Lucas rubbed his aching head. He had thought about it and thought about it, analyzing everything that had happened, trying to come up with a pattern and finding only more questions. Joan Mackenzie's death had resulted in people being afraid, outsiders paying attention to Jeneva's production, and Dana Sloe getting a part in the play. Were any of these the reason Joan had had to die? And then he and Kinny finding the mirror. Had that been accidental or somehow intended? And the results — him seeing Macbeth in the mirror; Kinny seeing things too, as well as learning to make wishes on it. That had led to her wish for Norris to get a better part, which in turn had brought about Alex's cruel death. Was Alex's death the ultimate reason why this whole inexplicable sequence of events had to occur? But if so, why?

And then, suddenly, Lucas remembered what Dana had said to Kinny after Alex's death — *Things of power.... You knew.* As if Kinny was somehow responsible. What if it was Kinny's *involvement* in Alex's death that was wanted.

Why? To make her feel guilty? That had certainly been the result. Kinny was carrying around so much guilt about Alex that sometimes Lucas worried she might never come out of it. And part of it – a lot of it – was his fault.

Kinny had made her wish for Lucas. Lucas hadn't asked for her to do it and would have done anything to undo the wish, but no amount of reasoning could let him forget that when she'd made that wish, she had done it to get him a part he wanted. He didn't want it once he got started in rehearsals. Not even with the freedom of Everett's direction could he find any new truths in Shakespeare's Macbeth. The only highlight of understudy rehearsals was the dagger scene, the one that Lucas had long ago figured out. That one remained true for Lucas because he knew that the real Macbeth had been as hopelessly trapped as the Macbeth of that scene in the play. But now nothing else in the play worked for Lucas. He knew the real Macbeth too well to play the one Shakespeare had written.

He came away from rehearsals with a profound sense of failure. It was worse, far worse, because a man had died to get this part for him, and worst of all that the man wouldn't have died if Lucas could only have made himself share his mirror visions with Kinny. She had made her wish only because she wanted to free Lucas from what she saw as a dangerous obsession with the mirror. She wouldn't have made the wish at all if she hadn't been worried about him, and she would never have made that particular wish if he had told her it was Macbeth he kept going to the mirror to see.

He should have told her. She had told him what *she* saw. He should have told her. But he hadn't, and she had wished, and it hadn't stopped him from wanting to look in that mirror and a man was dead and Kinny could think only of the evil her wish had led to. That haunted her. It haunted Lucas too. It tied her to Lucas with the weight of a ball and chain around his neck.

Whether he wanted it or not she was his duty now. It was up to him to protect her from any further harm that might come from that wish she'd made.

One of the things he had to do was to try to keep it from her that he still went to the mirror. It was strange how drawn to the mirror he remained, because every time he managed to look in it now it disappointed him. Before, seeing the same scene over and over hadn't bothered him; he watched it like a detective searching for clues, and almost enjoyed the familiarity, like a great play known by heart. But now he wanted more. He wanted more scenes of Macbeth; he wanted to see him smile, just once; he wanted to know what had happened to him afterward.

Lucas had never had many friends. He had his work, and his reading; he lived in plays, and it was enough. But it wasn't enough now. He needed more. And the mirror, which could have given it, refused him.

"Good grief, Lucas, are you still here?" Norris demanded.

Lucas blinked. Everyone else was gone, and Norris was standing in the doorway of the breakfast room, looking in at him. "What? I —"

"It's almost eleven. Chuck just phoned. The bus will be picking us up at one. We're going to Dunsinane first. I'm supposed to tell everyone."

He was gone. Lucas dragged himself stiffly to his feet. Dunsinane. The real Macbeth had been there. He hadn't died there as Shakespeare had said, but he had lived there, and that was something. Maybe a place Macbeth had been would hold some ancient memory of him. Lucas didn't expect it, but he hadn't expected that a mirror could reach out to him with its vision of the man either. It was a chance, that was all. He went upstairs to pack.

🔯 🔯 🔯

THEY WERE STANDING ON what felt like the top of the world. All around them were only wind and distant hilltops and gray skies heavy as damp wool. A cairn of stones marked the summit of Dunsinane. Earthen ramparts ringed the hill, but they were so worn down they could almost not be seen as man-made. They were all that remained of the days when Dunsinane had been one of the real Macbeth's strongholds.

His men had strode those ramparts, Lucas thought. Macbeth himself might have stood here, staring as Lucas now stared across the valley to the distant green of Birnam Wood. He would have seen Malcolm's men gather on the hills above that wood. Lucas took deep lungsful of the cold Scottish wind. Macbeth had been here. Lucas could feel it.

Far, far below the turf-and-rock heights, below the sea of heather that ringed the hill, below the evergreen wood that edged the hill track, was the B-road down which the bus had brought them. It cut through the green and purple hills like a strand of yarn dropped by a cat. Lucas made out the tiny shapes of the people who had started the climb but changed their minds, meandering back to the bus parked in the drive of the farmhouse nearby.

"Looks like a Dinky toy I had as a kid," Norris Frye said, following Lucas' gaze. He was holding a guidebook open in one hand, massaging his neck tiredly with the other. "Nice up here, isn't it?"

"Nice and cold," Gwen Park said, huddling into her jacket. "I've got a thermos of coffee in the bus. Anybody want to join me?"

"I will," Jeneva said.

She headed downhill with Gwen, her back very erect, movements easy and graceful. "She could be on her way to a garden party," Adam grumbled. "Not a word about the fire all day, you'll notice."

"She always was a better actor than a director," Christine remarked, wandering over from the cairn she'd been exploring.

By habit, Lucas checked for Kinny. It was all right, she was still by herself, poking abstractedly at a stone. Dana had stayed on the bus instead of climbing the hill. Today was the first time she hadn't tried to stick to Kinny like a shadow on a bright day. Partly, he'd managed that, making sure Kinny had a window seat on the bus and he the seat next to her, with Norris and Gwen in front and Christine and Adam behind.

Lucas went over to join her where she crouched over the stone. "Everything okay, Kinny?"

"Fine," she said.

"You want to go back to the bus?"

"Not yet."

He hesitated, feeling he ought to help her, but not knowing how. Christine was arguing with Adam; Norris was studying his guidebook as he bent over the cairn. Kinny's finger stroked the rock in front of her. It was an ordinary stone, fist-sized, dull. He sat down beside her, hugging his knees to his chest. She was silent for so long that he almost gave up and left her again. "I've got something to ask you, Lucas," she said at last, her eyes on the stone. "It's about the mirror. I want to know why you keep looking in it."

He shifted uncomfortably. But he'd got them both into enough trouble by not telling her the whole truth before. "I don't know exactly. I like watching Macbeth. Each time I look I think I might see more of him. Even now, when we're here and it's back in Edinburgh with the other stage props, I –"

"It's not in Edinburgh." Flatly.

"Not in –?"

"It's here. Down there, really. On the bus."

He blinked at her. "Why would it be here?"

"Because someone wanted it here." She turned her eyes on him then. "That should tell you something. Alex's death should tell you something. Your own burned hand should tell you something. But you don't listen! The mirror's dangerous, Lucas. Why don't you listen?"

"I'm not afraid of it," he said, as steadily as he could manage. "It doesn't give *me* any wishes."

"Have you asked it for any?"

"No!" He paused, modulated his voice, tried again. "Kinny, I look in the mirror because I want to know things. I don't care about the mirror itself. It's what it shows me —"

"What does it show you? That a man named Macbeth went into a stone circle one day, interrupted an old Hag's spell and sent her into the future in the mirror. Great." Her voice was shaking. He started to say something, but she stopped him with a look. "I'm trying to figure this out, Lucas. I've got to figure it out. You look in that mirror and you see the same thing over and over. So why go back? Once, fine, I can understand that; twice; even three or four times. But you keep on looking. Why? Why won't you stop?"

"You don't understand! I don't see it from a distance, the way you did that time. I see it...as if I *am* him. It's his memory I keep tapping into in the mirror, Kinny. I can tell you exactly what happened to Macbeth that night; what people said to him, what he saw, what he thought, what he said. 'Two into one. Find through this glass a future for thy past, that the name of Macbeth be not forgotten!' That's what he said to send the Hag into the future. And my hand. It wasn't the mirror that burned it. *My* hand hurt because of Macbeth's memory of it burning *his* hand. I'm that close to him! Don't you see?"

"No. I don't see. Tapping into his memory might have made you feel his pain, but it wouldn't actually burn your hand. And your hand was burnt."

He made a fist around the odd shininess that still remained in the skin of his palm even after more than a month, and was silent. Kinny scanned his face. After a long moment she turned away, biting hard on her bottom lip.

A soft rain began to fall. Christine squealed; Adam put his jacket over his head; Norris shoved his guidebook into his pocket and joined the others. "We're going back to the bus, Lucas," Christine called. "You two coming?"

"We'll catch up in a minute," he called back.

Kinny was already on her feet. For a moment she stood there over him while he peered up at her like a child. "Did it ever occur to you, Lucas," she said with desperate deliberation, "that it might be more than Macbeth's memories that are in that mirror?"

"What are you talking about?"

"I'm talking about Macbeth himself. All of him."

"All of...? I don't...."

She shook her head. "No, you don't, do you?" Wearily. "What I'm saying, Lucas, is that Macbeth might actually be in the mirror. The same way the Hag —"

He scrambled erect. "Macbeth, in the mirror? He can't be!"

"Why not? The Hag is in there."

"Not *still*. I mean, she was, but —"

"Macbeth sent her in the mirror into the future. This is the future. The mirror's here."

"That doesn't mean the Hag's still in it." His thoughts were whirling. He took a deep breath to calm himself. "That mirror could have materialized any time in the last nine hundred years and just aged normally till now. And the Hag knows how to come and go behind the glass. Why wouldn't she just come out?"

"I don't know why. I just know she hasn't. All I know is that she's in there now. I've seen her, Lucas. She's in there. I know it."

Lucas could hear his heart thudding. He couldn't keep still. His clenched right fist hammered the palm of his other hand. He strode away from her, turned, strode back. If the Hag really was in there, why not Macbeth, too? Macbeth had as good as taken the young girl's place when he intervened in the Hag's spell. The girl had been going to join the Hag behind the glass for the transfer. If Macbeth really had taken her place.... Why had he never thought of it? All that hypothesizing about visions of history and trapped memories!

Macbeth, the real Macbeth, inside the mirror, accessible....

"You said the mirror was on the bus," he said abruptly to Kinny. "Who has it?"

"I don't know," she said, drawing back.

"How do you know it's there, then?

"I can feel it."

"Where? Near where we're sitting? Where?"

"I told you, I don't know. Even if I did, I wouldn't tell you. I tried to make you understand, but you just want to look in that mirror even more."

"Is it Dana who has it?"

"I don't know. I DON'T KNOW!"

"But you must! How can you —?"

He broke off, realizing all of a sudden how close she was to crying. It was his job to look after Kinny, not to badger her. "Sorry," he muttered. But tears were already overflowing her eyes, joining with the raindrops on her cheeks. "Hey," he said, "hey, Kinny, I didn't mean to...."

She was crying quietly with her head erect and her lips tightly shut. Now and then a sound escaped her, a hopeless little sigh of misery that came from somewhere so deep and lost inside her that Lucas was sure he could never reach it. He had never seen anyone so lonely.

He felt wetness on his own cheeks. Rain. Only rain. Grief and guilt and rain over Dunsinane; he was responsible, she was. Pity for her washed over him. He took a deep breath, let it out again, took another. Gently, very gently, he put an arm around her shoulders.

"I'm sorry," he said. "Kinny, I'm so sorry."

A bus horn hooted faintly, summoning the

Macbeth company back to its well-planned schedule.

Lucas shook himself, and her with him. "Time to get on," he said.

Kinny stirred. "All right." It was a sigh rather than a voice.

His hand tightened on her wet jacket, and he began to steer her toward the hill track. She huddled a little closer to him, a weight under his arm, wearying.

Anyone looking at them from down in the bus would have thought they were in love.

Down in the bus.

Lucas squinted through the rain. The mirror was down in the bus. If he could find it...if Macbeth was in it....

Down there, in the bus, somewhere.

Chapter Fifteen

"THANK YOU FOR YOUR PROMPTNESS, ladies and gentlemen. We are now leaving Glamis Castle, but if you'll look out the coach windows to your left you will be rewarded with a last breathtaking view of this magnificent childhood home of the Queen Mother."

"I can't see a thing through this rain," Christine complained.

She said it very loudly, but the tartan-skirted tour guide continued speaking monotonously into her microphone, making no response.

"As you look, perhaps you could try to count the windows. If you see more outside than we could find inside, you'll know why there is a legend of a secret room, where the wicked Earl Beardie plays dice with the devil. Your driver Ronnie and I hope you found some hint of your friend Macbeth in Duncan's Hall —"

"You'd better learn not to call the Thane that, Mrs. Smythe, " Adam called. "We've got enough bad luck in this company."

"— on our drive to Forfar you will note that this fertile, quiet land, the heartland of

Macbeth's fortune, would not have been easily defensible when Malcolm invaded —"

"Does the woman never shut up?" Lucas muttered to Kinny, who was staring out the window into the misty afternoon.

"She doesn't bother me," Kinny told him simply.

It was true. Mostly, she didn't listen. When she did, she was grateful for the distraction. There were too many worse things on her mind to let a loquacious tour guide disturb her.

"Our next stop — and the last for the day — will be at the bustling town of Forfar, where we will spend the night. There are no direct links with Macbeth in Forfar, but his enemy Malcolm had a stronghold there where he was said to —"

Lucas groaned. He sat close enough to Kinny that when the bus jolted them against each other she could feel his body hard as an iron spring. Tight, she thought fearfully, too tight; he'd grown more and more tense since Dunsinane. She should never have told him the mirror was on the bus.

Why had she? She had been asking herself that question all afternoon. Why had she brought up the subject of the mirror at all? It had been a mistake. Another mistake. She had made so many. Sooner or later she'd have to pay for them all.

She closed her eyes and saw what she always

saw in unguarded moments — Alex lying dead, a girl, a Hag. The girl had her face turned away from Kinny. She always did, but her hair was honey-coloured and long, familiar except for the white blossoms in it. Power hovering, a mirror, something to say and to do....

Kinny forced her eyes open. Suddenly she was furious. Everything that had happened to her since she'd told her parents about National Theatre School seemed all at once part of some huge conspiracy, a plan designed to take advantage of what she was, to make her react so that eventually she'd be here on this bus going toward something she couldn't bear to think of. Trapped, no way out, responsible for someone's death and how could you pay for that?

How could you not?

"...the Forfar bridle," droned the tour guide, "used as a gag during seventeenth century witch-burnings...."

Outside the bus the rain sleeted down, cold as a Canadian November.

🔯 🔯 🔯

THE NEXT MORNING Lucas awoke early in his little room in the Forfar Inn. Kitchen sounds directly below him vied with the energetic noises of pre-breakfast deliveries. He was tired and on edge; he had hardly slept. The need to hold the mirror again had grown so much since yesterday that it would have worried him, if there hadn't been such a good explanation for it. If the essence of the real Macbeth was in the mirror, if Kinny was right, if the man Lucas had wondered about and thought about for so long was actually within reach....

But why did Lucas keep seeing only one of Macbeth's memories over and over, when that time in the second hand store he had seen something different? Surely the man in the mirror wasn't now thinking about that scene all the time, and in exactly the same way! No, it must be because Lucas was now holding the mirror differently. Macbeth wouldn't have held it by the sides; he would have grasped it firmly by the handle. What if Lucas held it that way?

A real man, thinking real thoughts, in that mirror. Lucas might be able to think them with him, just by holding onto the handle properly. It was a frightening thought, but exhilarating too. Other people had held the mirror by the handle and not known Macbeth's thoughts. Only he had known them. Only he had a strong enough link to the man to be able to tune in to his memories.

But first things first. Lucas had to get hold of the mirror. He had a pretty good idea who had it, but how he was to get it away from her was something else again.

He checked his watch, picked up his bedside

phone, dialed Kinny's room number, and let it ring. "Your morning wake-up call," he said, when her sleepy voice answered.

"Um."

"It's stopped raining. There's even some sun. Did you sleep all right?"

"The usual."

"Do you think you could eat breakfast with Gwen or Chrissie today? I'm going out."

"Sure. But what are you —?"

"Save me a seat on the bus."

He threw on some clothes, dumped the rest of his things in his suitcase, and headed down the stairs. He had decided to find himself a quiet spot out near the bus where he could watch what people did with their luggage. Maybe Dana would leave hers by the storage compartment of the bus instead of supervising its loading personally. If she did, and if her case wasn't locked....

Even this early, Forfar was a lively little town. People were doing their morning shopping or walking their dogs. The clatter of their footsteps and the soft burr of their conversation echoed in the cobbled street lined solid with ancient buildings. It was disconcerting to see how many of the buildings were spray-painted with slogans. Lucas saw "Scotland for Scots" and "English out." It reminded him of home, only in his neighbourhood the graffiti was mostly anti-French, kids without accents coming in from the suburbs and painting "French-kissoff" all over the factories. It was the same in Quebec now, Kinny had told him, only the words were *"Anglais, efface!"* Every group seemed to have its own vision of itself as a unified whole, and was determined to make that vision true even if it meant shutting out part of what it was.

The bus was parked down the street from the hotel in a spot wide enough for it to turn around. But right out in front of the hotel there was an empty luggage cart labeled with a Canadian flag and the words MACBETH COMPANY. Funny how nobody but actors seemed to mind using Macbeth's name. Lucas laid his suitcase on the cart, then bought a newspaper and took it to a bench in a patch of sunlight nearby. He opened the newspaper and waited behind it.

The patch of sun had gone and the air had turned cold and damp when the first of the company came out from the hotel. It was Kinny with Gwen and Brian Able. "Another balmy August day in Scotland," Gwen said, dropping her cases on the cart and buttoning up her coat.

"We're as far north as Alaska, here," Brian pointed out.

They headed for the bus without seeing Lucas. A whole crowd came out next, including

Christine and Adam and half a dozen other people who weren't in the company. Jeneva trailed them, speaking over her shoulder to someone still inside the hotel. Lucas strained behind his paper to see if it was Dana. People were in the way, but Jeneva was using her actor's voice, and Lucas heard every word. "It's quite all right, Mrs. Maugham, we have lots of room, and it won't take us out of our way at all. We're going right into Elgin. The real King Duncan was killed there, but of course you'll know that, living in this area yourself. We're interested in everything to do with the play."

The woman she was talking to was out of the door now, though someone nearer to Lucas was leaning sideways and blocking her top half from his view. He saw an expensive pair of brogues, a long shapeless skirt, a liver-spotted claw-like hand, a purse.

"I am very grateful to you," the woman said, her voice very old and very cultured and with just the faintest hint of impatience in it.

Lucas frowned, letting the newspaper fall into his lap. Familiarity itched at him. He wasn't sure, but he thought he might have heard that voice before. Or not exactly that voice, but close....

The crowd thinned. The person blocking his view of Jeneva's new acquaintance moved away. Lucas stared and stared, his mouth so dry he couldn't even swallow.

A face channeled with wrinkles, lips wide and loose over newly fitted false teeth, beautiful white hair done in a careful bun, a thrusting widow's hump....

He must have made some sound. Blue-gray eyes swiveled his way. Aghast, he met them with his own; he had no choice. Jeneva chatted on. Suitcases thudded into the luggage cart. Somebody laughed. Adam and Christine continued to bicker.

They didn't know, Lucas thought. The hunchback was here, and they thought she was just an ordinary old woman.

She'd been there the day Joan was electrocuted. She'd been there the day Alex died. She'd been there when the fire broke out. And now she was here, out in the open and coming on the bus.

"Right this way, Mrs. Maugham," Jeneva said. "Just leave your case on the cart. Our driver will take care of it."

"I'll carry it," the woman replied. "I don't like to cause trouble."

"Then let me," Jeneva said.

"Thank you, but it's practically empty. I can manage."

With all the assurance in the world she walked beside Jeneva to the bus. Lucas followed her with his eyes, half getting to his feet to watch her as long as possible. His heart pounded. Say something. She's dangerous. Don't let her get on the bus. Stop her.

I don't like to cause trouble, she had said. And her eyes, staring right at him, had said, *But I will, if you try to stop me.*

She was on the bus. It was too late. Who would have believed him, anyway? He turned away, his knees trembling. And there in front of him was Dana, standing by the luggage cart with her suitcases in her hands.

She gazed at him, enigmatic as a sphynx. "This is Scotland, you know, Lucas, not downtown Chicago. You don't have to guard luggage on a public street here."

"Do you know about...her?" The question jolted out of him. He wouldn't have asked it if he hadn't been so shocked.

"Mrs. Maugham?" Dana asked carelessly. "We had breakfast with her. The Grampians' bus service went on strike this morning. She'd have been stuck here if Jeneva hadn't offered her a lift."

Of course Dana knew about her. She and that woman were partners. Dana could pretend all she liked, but his time for that was over. "Do you have the mirror, or does she?"

Her eyes glittered at him. She seemed to be considering whether or not to answer him. "That mirror is not your concern," she said at last.

"You don't know that. You don't know what

I see in that mirror. *Who* I see. You don't –"

"Oh, but I do know. I know exactly. I also know that you have made him important to you, when he doesn't have the faintest idea of your existence. Listen to me," she said, and he was startled at the naked sincerity in her voice. "You are in very great danger. Nothing in that mirror is worth what you will pay, if you take it in your hands once more."

"I don't like threats," Lucas said defiantly.

"It's not a threat," she said. "It's a warning. Listen to it."

"You don't scare me."

Her eyes went very cold and hard. "Very well. Have it your own way. I don't scare you. You don't listen. You'll do what you want, and we'll do what we must."

He fell back, his hand involuntarily clutching his chest. Under his shirt the iron medallion flared hot as pain. Somehow he managed to lift his chin. Somehow he got his shoulders square and his body moving. Turn. Step. Step. Go.

On the steps of the bus he stopped and glared over his shoulder at her. She was looking after him as expressionlessly as if he wasn't even there.

❈ ❈ ❈

"...MOUNT BATTOCK IN THE DISTANCE. Not the highest of the Grampians, which have eroded over the ages to only one-third their original height, but respectable nonetheless, wouldn't you say?" Mrs. Smythe tittered, as if she had just been very witty. "Here, of course, we are traversing a much more hospitable area, the Howe of the Mearns, named for...."

The tour guide's words flowed over Kinny's head. Listen, she told herself, listen to the words, don't think about that woman sitting hunched into her cardigan in the seat beside Jeneva, don't think of Dana across the aisle from you, just listen.

"...contrasting with the heights, where the vegetation is mainly heather, blaeberry and cowberry. Our route today will not take us through the mountains, but do not despair —" another titter "— we will see some heather nonetheless. No doubt you will be interested to know that the only true Scottish heather is the pale purple ling which blooms —"

"Excuse me, Mrs. Smythe," Jeneva called to the tour guide. "Are we at all near —" She broke off, looked a question at the woman beside her.

"North Water Bridge," Mrs. Maugham said pleasantly.

"North Water Bridge?" Jeneva repeated, more loudly.

The tour guide turned to the driver. "Ronnie?"

"Five minutes from here," he said laconically over his shoulder.

"Good," Jeneva said. "Mrs. Maugham has been telling me of an alternate route to Elgin which will avoid the main roads and let us see something of the mountains. It's just past North Water Bridge."

"The B974," Ronnie grunted, nodding.

Mrs. Smythe pushed her glasses higher on her nose. "We can't take an alternate route, Miss Strachan. We're booked into an inn at Aberdeen for lunch."

"We'll telephone to cancel, the first phone booth we see."

"But —"

"I realize it's a nuisance, Mrs. Smythe, and I'm very sorry to cause you difficulties, but as you know we're interested in anything to do with the era of the play, and it turns out that this particular road is a very ancient one —"

"Some people call it the old drovers' road," Mrs. Maugham put in, her teeth clacking faintly. "It's been in use since the time of Macbeth. People say Macbeth himself used it, fleeing from Malcolm in the years after Dunsinane."

"She wants us to go that way," Lucas said softly to Kinny.

"Yes."

"They have a plan. That hunchback and

Dana and the third sister, whoever she is. I heard them say so, back in Stratford. I think this is part of it."

"Yes," Kinny said again. It was all she could manage.

"You two got your heads together again?" Adam said, leering over his shoulder at them. "Quite the pair of lovebirds, aren't we?"

"Shut up, Adam," Lucas said almost violently. "Norris, give me your guide book for a minute, will you?"

Without a word, Norris handed it over while Adam grinned unrepentently. Lucas flipped impatiently through the map index. "Grampian Highlands," he muttered, "North Water Bridge, page 91."

Kinny folded her hands tightly in her lap, pressed her lips together, and concentrated on breathing.

"Hey, Kinny, your name's on this map," Lucas said suddenly.

A brochure in a pink-and-white bedroom in Stratford. *If some very powerful event happened near a place long ago and you gave the name of that place to a child....* She had known. She had known it the moment the hunchback had made Jeneva suggest the alternate route.

"Look, Kinny, here it is — Kincardine O'Neil." She glanced at the map quickly, to satisfy him. "The B974 goes practically there." He frowned, his moving finger stopping suddenly at another village very near Kincardine O'Neil. "Lumphanan. I know that name." His voice dropped to a mutter. "Why do I —?"

Kincardine O'Neil. Lumphanan. Macbeth.

"I remember," he breathed. "I remember now." He turned to her. "There's a stone circle near Lumphanan," he said. "I read about it in a book back in Stratford. It was at that stone circle that —"

"I know," Kinny said. "Don't talk about it. That's where we're going. Don't talk."

"You know for sure we're going there?"

"There's our turnoff," she said, staring out the window. The bus turned the corner onto the B974.

Two seats up and across the aisle, Jeneva was talking. "We'll need to stop somewhere for lunch. Do you know of a decent restaurant in the area, Mrs. Maugham?"

"The Gordon Arms is very pleasant. It's in a lovely little village right on the Dee, only a mile or two off the main road. Your company would enjoy it, Miss Strachan. Macbeth stayed just outside that village in the days before he met his end, and Malcolm camped there."

"Then of course we must see it," Jeneva said. "The Gordon Arms, did you say? What's the name of the village?"

Kinny took a shaky breath. Lucas clasped

her hand. They both stared straight ahead.

"It's named after the family that once owned the land," Mrs. Maugham said. "The Neils, they were. The village is called Kincardine O'Neil."

Chapter Sixteen

THE GRAMPIAN MOUNTAINS WERE WIND-swept and empty, a wide-sky loneliness of treeless purple crags. The road ribboned uncertainly below them. Kinny marked the journey by bridges. She memorized them one by one, tiny stone bridges arching over flurries of streams in the shadow of Bronze Age cairns, others with names Norris read out with relish from his guide-book: Clatterin' Brig, Spital Cott Bridge, the Bridge of Dye. This last was actually two bridges, one ancient and abandoned, the other modern but very narrow, triumphing over the down-pouring water under the ruined gaze of a house on the hilltop. Just four walls and a chimney were left of that house, a stony piece of jetsam half buried in heather and open to the storms that scoured this landscape half a dozen times a week. No animals, no people, not even a bird to fly overhead. Just unbearable loneliness and the sheer drop down to the perilous waters of Glen Dye.

Some people can swim in it, some people immerse themselves and drown.

A great evergreen forest pressed in on the road beyond Glen Dye. Many found it a relief after the emptiness of the heights. Kinny didn't. The thick darkness made her feel as if there wasn't enough air to breathe, and the number of dead rabbits on the road nauseated her. She had had more than she could stand by lunch time, more than she could stand of Jeneva's nose-to-nose conversations with the toothy Mrs. Maugham, more than she could stand of Dana watching her while Lucas kept a wary eye on them both and Kincardine O'Neil drew nearer and nearer.

"Getting excited to see your namesake, Kinny?" Norris asked once, over his shoulder.

"Not exactly," she answered stiffly.

Norris looked at her, made a face that said, what's the matter with *her*, and turned around huffily in his seat again.

"It's really bothering you, going there, isn't it?" Lucas said quietly.

"Yes."

"An hour or two, that's all we'll be spending there." Silence. "Just enough time to eat, and maybe wander around a little." Silence. "Is it because the hunchback suggested it? It may just be a coincidence, isn't it? Isn't that right? Kinny?"

"Right, right," she muttered.

It wasn't, of course. But she couldn't tell Lucas what she now was sure was going to happen. If he knew, he would be bound to think he had to stop it. It wouldn't matter to him that it was something she had brought on herself, something that blood and honour and peace-of-mind and the terror of committing evil in the future all made necessary. He would simply step in and offer to protect her, and the terrible thing was that she might be so weak that she'd let him.

It was doubly frightening because if he tried to help her he would be in great danger. People had died to manoeuvre Kinny into having to do what the Hag wanted. Joan's death had got Dana into the acting company and into the same house with Kinny; and Alex's death... Kinny swallowed hard. That death was her responsibility. A death for a wish, a blood debt that had to be paid. Kinny knew, but Lucas did not, and if he interfered, the hunchback might do anything. It would never occur to Lucas that he might be her next victim. It would be like that mirror; he knew it was dangerous, and it didn't change anything.

Kinny turned right away from him, staring out the window at the rich green darkness of the Stewdrum Forest. She felt him withdraw in return, offended by her rebuff. But it was for his own good. He wouldn't see that, any more than he'd see the reason why the Hag would have to be set free from her glass prison, leaving Macbeth to stay alone in it forever. But it had to be done, all the same.

"The River Dee at last," Norris said, brandishing his guidebook, as the road came out into the open, paralleling a wide, beautiful river to their right. Sunlight glittered on its tranquil surface. All traces of the early morning clouds were gone.

"Where do we cross?" Adam asked.

"A place called Hunter. As far as I can tell, that's this hotel right here."

"I'm starving," Adam said, looking longingly at the hotel.

"The Gordon Arms is only another five minutes," the attentive Mrs. Maugham told him.

They made a sharp turn onto the bridge. "The River Dee is one of the best salmon rivers in Scotland," came a voice from the microphone.

Mrs. Smythe had finally found something in her official notes to correspond with their altered route.

The last bridge, Kinny thought.

My last bridge.

She rested her forehead against the window glass, and tried not to be sick.

🏵 🏵 🏵

DESPITE LUCAS' MISGIVINGS about anything Mrs. Maugham was willing to recommend, the

Gordon Arms Hotel *was* a good place to eat. The building was only a few centuries old, but clearly it was the focal point of Kincardine O'Neil. The hotel proper was a large stone building with twin chimneys surmounting a round-windowed gable, and it had an older-looking, single storey attachment, dormered and turreted. Inside, the dining room and bar were just shy of elegant, with brown velvet curtains, warm wood floors and good china on the tables.

Kinny pointed at random to something on the menu, and the waitress brought fried camembert, apologizing cheerfully for the lack of gooseberry sauce. It didn't matter, Lucas thought, because she didn't eat it anyway. He himself had skipped breakfast, and not even the presence of Dana and the hunchbacked Mrs. Maugham could take away his appetite. He wolfed down a delicious slice of steak and mushroom pie and a huge bowl of trifle; then, while Kinny was in the washroom, he wandered around the dining room and hall, examining the extensive display of maps and photos.

The photographs were about a century old, but they showed little change from what he himself had observed as the bus had driven down the main street of the village. The buildings were gray stone darkened with age, dignified despite additions such as electrical cables and plumbing stacks and discreet modern signs. Nowadays, as in the time of the photographs, there were hardly any commercial establishments — a general store combined with a post office, a hairdresser, a single clothing store, the hotel. Almost nothing remained to indicate Kincardine O'Neil's twelfth century prosperity as the famous meeting place of the North-South and East-West roads.

The exact place of the crossroads was apparently here, where the hotel now stood. Lucas went to the front door and stared out, but he could see no obvious North-South road, just a rutted dirt track starting across the street from the hotel. He checked it on the map, and saw that it ended at the River Dee. A bridge had stood there once, built in the early 1200s. There had been a hospice for travellers, too, but that also was gone. The church that had been attached to the hospice was still there — they had passed it in the bus — but it had lost its heather-thatched roof in 1740, Mrs. Smythe had told them. It was strange to be a tourist in a village that had dealt with more tourists eight hundred years ago than it did now.

On their way into the hotel Mrs. Smythe had again used her resource books to show them St. Erchard's Well, right next door. There was no visible water, and it was hard to make out the carvings on the ancient stone surround, but if

Mrs. Smythe was right it was the oldest thing in the village. St. Erchard had been the patron saint of the parish in the time of Macbeth's great-great-grandfather, Malcolm I of Scotland. Another of Malcolm I's many descendants was Malcolm Canmore, who defeated Macbeth and became king in his place.

Macbeth had fled here, Lucas thought soberly, here to this important and prosperous place where people were civilized and venerated their saints and their kings and knew how to treat travellers. And it hadn't done any good, because Malcolm had caught up with him. Three interminable years of fighting and running and making stands and fighting again, and all of it for nothing, all of it leading only to bloodshed and death on the hills just north of this village. When Macbeth's forces were decimated and his friends were gone, there was nowhere new left to go, no new choices to make, nothing to be done but to take up an ancient promise and beg the help of a Hag and a Mother and a Maiden. And they had refused. They had stood in their circle of stone, and they had refused.

Lucas continued to pore over the map. About halfway between Lumphanan and Torphins there was a tiny mark with an equally tiny label. He bent near. *Stone circle.* His breath caught in his throat. He scanned the rest of the map minutely, but no other stone circle was indicated. He used his index finger to measure the distance from Kincardine O'Neil, comparing it to the scale. Two miles, maybe; a little more. No distance at all, even in those days.

"Is that the one?" Kinny asked, her voice paper-thin.

"Yes. I think so. Yes." She was standing behind him, peering over his shoulder. He turned to her, hardly noticing her pinched look, hardly looking at her at all. "I want to see that stone circle."

"Mmm."

"It's not too far. We could walk it and be back in two hours, tops, even overland. But Mrs. Smythe said we'd be leaving at three. If we could rent bikes – borrow them, maybe – nobody would lend a car to somebody they'd never met, but a bike –"

Jeneva appeared at the door of the dining room. She was with the bus driver Ronnie, and she looked upset. "Ladies and gentlemen," she announced, "we've got a tiny problem. Ronnie has just come back from trying to take the bus to the filling station. He can't get it to start. The mechanic's come, and apparently the problem's not going to be simple to fix."

Lucas stared at Kinny. She refused to meet his eyes.

"It wouldn't be simple to fix," Christine said to

Adam, but loud enough for everyone to hear. "Not if it's got anything to do with *our* company."

Jeneva sent a smoking look Christine's way. "We might have to order special parts. That could take some time."

"Days maybe," Ronnie put in gloomily. "Probably closer to a week."

"We don't have a week," Meredith Archer said. "We have to be back in Edinburgh to open on Monday."

Jeneva's voice was very calm. "Everything's in hand. Mrs. Smythe has called the tour company, and they're going to send us a replacement bus —"

"That's all right, then," Meredith said relievedly.

"— as soon as they can. The problem is, there isn't a spare one available, not until tomorrow. So we're going to have to stay here overnight."

She looked at the hunchbacked woman, who was sitting very still over a piece of cheese, hands folded in her lap. "Mrs. Maugham, I'm so sorry. I know you were hoping to get to Elgin this afternoon."

Mrs. Maugham smiled gently. "Please don't worry about me."

Norris said cheerfully, "At least the food's good here. What about rooms? Does this place have enough for us, Jeneva?"

"Not quite. But there's a bed-and-breakfast

at the east end of the village. Norton House, it's called – we passed it on our way in. It's supposed to be very nice. I was hoping some of you younger folk would stay there, since this hotel is the only place to eat and it's a fair walk from there. Two doubles available. Any volunteers?"

"I'll go," Kinny said. Her face was very white.

"Me too," Lucas put in automatically.

"Someone to share with Kinny?" Jeneva asked.

"I wouldn't mind –" Dana began.

"No, no, Dana, I know you're probably in better shape than the rest of us put together, but I'm sure someone else will be delighted. Christine?"

Christine shrugged. "I suppose I could. And I'll bet Adam would love to share with Lucas."

"That's settled, then," Jeneva said. "Thank you all very much. You can pick up your keys at the desk and your luggage at the bus. If anybody needs me in the next little while, I'll be on the phone to Stratford."

She threw a brilliant smile to the company at large, turned efficiently on her heel, and disappeared.

"Thanks a lot, Chrissie," Adam said, deeply sarcastic.

"You should be grateful to me," she answered.

"There's nothing but bad luck for anyone who has to be near Jeneva Strachan. Deaths, accidents, terrible reviews, and broken-down buses. I personally will sleep a whole lot better at the other end of the village from her."

Lucas took Kinny by the hand. "Come on."

He intended to be the first one there when the luggage was unloaded from the bus. He knew now what Dana's suitcases looked like. If he had anything to say about it there was going to be another little accident in Kincardine O'Neil today, only this time it was going to be to the hinges of Dana's cases. It worried him a little that Dana didn't hurry out after him. She must have known what he intended to do, but she didn't seem in the slightest bit disturbed about it. He didn't like the way she casually wandered over to Mrs. Maugham's table as they were leaving.

Those two were responsible for disabling the bus. He was certain of it. He didn't know how they'd done it; he just knew they had.

"You guessed, didn't you?" Lucas said to Kinny when they were safe outside. "Even on the bus you knew we wouldn't be leaving here at three."

She looked at him dully. "We can go to the stone circle now."

"Now that we have a choice, I wouldn't mind going a bit later. With moonlight, it'd be more like the way I saw it in —"

"I want to go now."

There was no arguing with her. "Okay," he said, shrugging. "But there's something I have to do first." There was a heap of suitcases already standing by the bus. Obviously Ronnie had unloaded them while Jeneva was making arrangements with the hotel. Lucas wished he'd come out sooner.

"The mirror's not there," Kinny said, obviously figuring out what he had in mind.

He scrutinized her suspiciously. How had she known what he was planning to do? And was she telling the truth, or was she just trying to prevent him from looking in the mirror again?

"Women have handbags, Lucas," she burst out suddenly and angrily. "Do you really think anybody'd store something as important as that mirror in a suitcase when it could go in a handbag and stay right under your arm all the time?"

He grimaced involuntarily. She was right. "Sorry," he muttered. "I've been stupid." She was looking at the ground and he wondered if she had even heard him. He squared his shoulders. "I suppose we should take our stuff to Norton House." She didn't answer. "I'd like to get a decent map of this area, too." Still she didn't answer. All of a sudden he'd had it.

"Listen," he blurted resentfully, "if you think you're the only one under pressure from all this....What's bugging you, anyway? These last few days you've been acting as if you're living your last moments on Earth. I'm sick of coddling you. I'm sick of looking after you. I'm sick to bloody well death of keeping you away from people like Dana."

Her head jerked up. He was shocked to his core at the terror in her face. "Maybe I'm sick to bloody well death of you doing it," she got out, trying for outrage and barely managing a whisper. "I never asked you to look after me. I never asked you to do anything for me. So just stop doing it. Stop doing it now."

And she marched away from him, away from the heap of luggage, away from the bus and the hotel; a solitary, thin figure with her hands in her pockets and her shoulders hunched, heading for sunset down the thousand-year-old East-West Road.

Chapter Seventeen

H
E TOOK HER SUITCASE DOWN TO NORTON
House along with his own. It was a
stately old stone home whose back
garden went forever. The only obvious entrance
was at the back off a huge circular gravel drive.
He knocked; a woman came to the door, wiping her hands on an apron. "You must be from
that theatre group," she said, smiling in a
friendly way. "Come in, come in."

He returned her smile in as sincere a way as
he could manage with the way he'd treated
Kinny still fresh in his mind. His hostess was
the rare kind of person who didn't ask a lot of
questions. After showing him to his room and
telling him where to put Kinny's suitcase, she
went back to her own business in the kitchen.

He didn't bother to unpack. Something was
seriously and dreadfully wrong in Kinny's life.
It was more than guilt over that wish she had
made. She knew that something terrible was
coming; she didn't just fear it, she actually
knew. He hadn't fully realized it until she had
turned that despairing face toward him at the
bus just now. But even her obvious misery hadn't
stopped him telling her how sick he was of

looking after her. All these weeks of trying to show Kinny she had him to rely on, and now he had cut the ties between them as ruthlessly as if he had physically shoved her away.

Urgency possessed him. He had to find Kinny and try to make his peace with her. He had to do it *now*.

She had been heading west. There were towns to the west of Kincardine O'Neil, but there was no reason for her to have gone to any of them. It was the stone circle she had wanted to see. She had stood and looked over his shoulder at the map on the hotel wall after lunch; she would know the two ways to get to the circle. Both began at the same place – a little northward-bearing road across from the filling station at the west end of town. One route followed that road the whole way, angling across the countryside until it came out to the east of Lumphanan right where the map marked the stone circle. The other way followed the same route for a while, but left it to cut north along a footpath to Lumphanan, from where another road went east to the stone circle.

Lucas was sure Kinny would be heading for the stone circle, though there was no way to tell which of the two routes she would take. He decided to use one route to get there and the other one returning, and tossed a coin to decide which to take first. The footpath won.

He hurried through the village to the gas station, then headed up the road. After a little while the road veered to the right and he saw the footpath branching north. He took it.

If he had been in any other mood, the countryside would have been exhilarating, full of brambles and broom, with grouse trotting like cartoon road-runners under a white-plumed blue sky. Even feeling as he did, a part of his brain noticed the beauty, thistles with their seed parachutes, the purple spikes of willow herb, pine forest, dense and dark, the wind soughing and the gleam of birches. He seemed to be always climbing. Open pasture, fieldstone walls, bales of hay, a dirt track through bracken. Higher still, colonies of rabbits, dead birds on the ground, a shotgun casing in the path, an old man with a sheepdog. Lucas asked him if he had seen Kinny. "Young, fair, pretty, wearing jeans," he described swiftly.

"Young? Ach no," the shepherd replied slowly. "Happen 'a saw anoother, but she were no' tha' young, an' no' wearin' troowsers."

Then a short section of paved track, a dip to houses, doves, the musky smell of sheep. Up once more, and finally, the view into Lumphanan valley — a gentle green lowland dominated by a ring of trees containing a strange flat-topped mound, very large and clearly man-made.

He took a side trip to it because anybody seeing that pudding-shaped mound would have gone to check it out. Kinny wasn't there though. No one was. There was a signpost announcing what the mound was — The Peel of Lumphanan — with a detailed history of the earth-palisaded fortress it had once been. There was a whole separate section about Macbeth. He had died here, the sign said. His head had been cut off against a stone three hundred metres to the southwest. His body had been buried on Perk Hill to the north.

Macbeth, dead? Slowly, unhappily, Lucas made his way to the stone the sign had mentioned. It was barely hip-high and had a flattish, undistinctive gray top streaked with bird-droppings. A pair of haws, red as drops of blood, had been placed on it, obviously deliberately. He touched the stone. Under his fingers it seemed dreadfully ordinary, warm from the sun, a little furry with lichen. He felt completely detached from it. Macbeth, decapitated here? Not his Macbeth. He couldn't believe it. He would feel something, if it were true.

But if there really were a body buried on Perk Hill....

No. Macbeth was in the mirror. Kinny thought he was, and Dana had hinted as much. His body couldn't — it simply couldn't — be buried where the sign said it was.

Lucas left Lumphanan and headed east toward the stone circle. It was all downhill, and he made good speed. The circle was supposed to be at the first crossroads east of the village, but when he got there there was no sign of any standing stones. The map had shown the words "stone circle" right on the highway, but when Lucas strained to remember, he thought the location dot might have been a little to the north of it. He went that way, the road passing almost immediately under an old railway bridge. A little way beyond that a very narrow laneway branched to the left, along which, some distance down, Lucas could glimpse the slate-topped roof and matching side chimneys of a typically Scottish house. There was a barn nearby. And in the tussocky, rough pasture between the buildings and himself was a stone circle.

It was one of the most derelict antiquities Lucas had ever seen. He thought it was stretching things to call it a circle at all. Of the original dozen or more stones, only four were left standing. The rest had fallen or been tipped over, some lying prone on the circumference of the ring and others scattered in fragments all over the place; most were surrounded by stinging nettles. The original ring had probably been no more than fifteen or twenty paces across, and now looked much smaller, reduced by the inward-falling stones. The air was permeated with the smell of cow dung.

The shapes of the stones still standing seemed familiar, but that was the only thing that did. If this was the imposing Goddess Ring Lucas had seen so often in the mirror, it was greatly changed. But there was nowhere else for that Goddess Ring to be. Either this was it, or the actual stone circle had somehow disappeared off the maps, or – he made himself face it – the Goddess Ring he had seen in the mirror had never have existed at all. But that would mean that everything the mirror had shown him was a lie, that there had been no transfer spell, no witches trying to possess a pretty young girl, no angry honourable man preventing it and getting caught up in the spell himself. In that case the sign at the Peel of Lumphanan was right, and Macbeth really might have been killed with the last of his forces away on the other side of Lumphanan, and his headless body buried on Perk Hill.

Which was the truth? Lucas wished he had never seen the sign. He had made a link to Macbeth through the mirror; he couldn't bear the idea that the link was false. If he went into that stone circle now and felt no hint of Macbeth there, it would mean either that Macbeth had indeed never been there, and that everything Lucas had believed for the last month was false, or that he had been there but Lucas couldn't recognize it. Either way, he would have been taken in.

I don't have to go into the circle, Lucas told himself. I don't have to know.

Kinny wasn't there, anyway, unless she was hiding. He called her name a few times, but there was no reply. If she had been to the stone circle at all, then she must have taken the other route both coming and going. That would explain why he hadn't met her. He looked at his watch. It was late. He had to go. He could come back and explore the circle another time, if he wanted to. Right now he had to find Kinny.

He took the road all the way back, half running, hoping to catch up to Kinny. But there was no sign of her. Once he heard something in a bramble thicket just off the road, a furtive rustle, a sound like someone trying not to cry. He stopped, calling Kinny's name. Nothing. He stepped off the road. A grouse whirred up at him. *Go back, go back, go back!* He jumped in surprise. "Kinny? Are you there?" Nothing. He walked on.

When he got to Kincardine O'Neil he was certain he would find her at the hotel, but she wasn't there. Norton House then. Surely she would be back by now.

But she wasn't. It was seven o'clock, and she wasn't there. "She hasn't been here since I checked in," Christine told Lucas, when he knocked on the door to ask. "I've been napping for the last little while, but I'd have known if she'd come in. There's her suitcase, though," she indicated the case that Lucas himself had put in the corner of the room more than five hours before "so at least you know she can find her way home. She's probably just gone for a walk. Did you hear about Jeneva?"

He wasn't interested in Jeneva. "Kinny didn't come into the hotel while you were there this afternoon?"

She raised her Renaissance eyebrows at him. "Isn't Kinny just a teeny bit...young for you, darling?"

He made an abrupt movement of distaste, badly disguised. "Sorry, but I've got to find Kinny."

He heard the door slam as he walked down the hall. Adam was splashing in the bathroom. Lucas recognized his voice, singing something about the "bea-eeu-tiful bri-iny sea." He knocked on the door.

The singing stopped. "Who is it?"

"Lucas. Sorry to bother you. Have you seen Kinny anywhere?"

"Not since lunch."

Maybe she was back at the hotel by now. He'd already checked once, but that was half an hour ago. Wherever she'd gone, she would have to pass the hotel on her way to Norton House. It was dinner time; she hadn't had any lunch; she must have stopped there; there wasn't anywhere else for her to be. In his room he pulled on a thick sweater. It caught on the iron chain around his neck, and he was too impatient to free it carefully. He jerked hard, felt something give, and cursed aloud. Constant wearing had bent some of the links of the chain, and his violent pull just now had finished the job. He dropped the broken chain and pendant on the dresser, zipped on a windproof jacket and headed out again.

In the growing twilight he strode along the highway toward the Gordon Arms. Cows were making their way toward the river in single file; the tangy aroma of woodsmoke filled the air. The roofless church was on fire with sunset, a pink glow lighting the ancient buttresses and warming even the gravestones. It was beautiful, but Lucas saw little of it. He had made the circuit of all the places Kinny could have been, and she still wasn't anywhere. If she wasn't in the hotel this time....

He strode into the warm, smoky fug of the Gordon Arms, his eyes searching every table and even the crowd at the bar, though she wasn't officially old enough to drink. His heart sank. She wasn't here.

"Have you seen Kinny?" he asked Norris and Meredith, who were leaning against the bar drinking red wine.

"Has she disappeared too?" Norris replied. "First Jeneva, and now —"

"Jeneva?" Christine had also mentioned Jeneva. "What's going on?"

"You know how she was going to phone Stratford this afternoon?" Lucas nodded impatiently. "Well, Chrissie overheard the call — you know Chrissie — it was about next year's list of shows. Anyway, the long and the short of it is, Jeneva's not going to be directing at Stratford next year. Chrissie says they don't want her back ever again."

"She's definitely out," Meredith put in, nodding soberly.

"But why?"

"Everything that's happened to this production is why," Norris said. "But that fire in the Assembly Hall was the final straw. Canadian Press reported the story today. All kinds of stuff about Canada's image being tarnished in the eyes of the world. That was enough for Stratford. My guess is it'll be enough for any decent theatre in the country. Odds are Jeneva's finished as a director in Canada."

"Did you say she's disappeared?" Lucas asked, frowning.

Meredith shook her head. "That's just Norris dramatizing. She went for a walk, that's all."

"She's been gone since three," Norris

said into his wine glass.

Since three. Kinny had been gone much longer than that.

"And she was wearing that stupid caftan and high heels," Norris added. "Nobody could walk for four hours dressed like that."

"She's probably found herself a little pub in some other village where she can be by herself," Meredith said. "I would if I were her."

The girl behind the bar gave a brisk wipe to a few square millimetres of space in front of Lucas, smiled at him and said, "Sorry I took so long. We're that busy. What can I get you, sir?"

"Nothing, thanks. Norris, where is Dana now?"

"She and that funny old Mrs. Maugham ordered a taxi from Aboyne and went sightseeing or something. They're not back yet. Where are you off to?"

Lucas gave a wild smile and slipped away.

Kinny was missing. Jeneva was missing. Dana and the hunchback were missing. Where Jeneva fit into all this, Lucas didn't know. What he did know, with a sudden sick and urgent certainty, was that there was only one place the other three could be.

Outside the hotel, darkness was falling fast. The moon, a near-circle of white light, was already visible in the eastern sky.

Lucas dug his elbows into his sides and ran.

Chapter Eighteen

THERE WERE STARS, BUT ONLY IN THE WEST-ern sky. The east was all moonlight. It glittered in Lucas' eyes as he ran, an unearthly brilliance that turned grass blades silver and painted black ghosts on the ground. He was panting; a stitch burned in his side. You're in good shape, he told himself, you don't need to rest, you're on a decent road, just *go*.

Bits and pieces fell into place with the thudding of his feet. There had been three witches — Maiden, Mother, and Hag, but only two were left after Macbeth had sent the Hag and the mirror into the future. Now, a thousand years later, there were three sisters — Dana, the hunchbacked 'Mrs. Maugham', and the third unseen sister who was in prison — and it would be a prison, wouldn't it, if you were inside a mirror in a body whose real-world form had already been too old a thousand years before? You couldn't come out from the mirror in your own body because it would disintegrate the moment it touched the real world, but in someone else's body, in a young girl's body, in Kinny's body....

God. Oh, God. Why hadn't he figured it out before this? Dana with her too-youthful frilly dresses and her round-eyed innocence gone hard, Mrs. Ha-Ha-Mom turned destroyer, both of them changed irrevocably by their long, long search for their sister the Hag. How could he have been so stupid? He had known right from the beginning that the hunchback and Dana were too interested in the mirror. Kinny had even told him the Hag was still in it. "She won't let us just take it and go," Dana had said to the hunchback that night on the island in Stratford. 'It' was the mirror; 'she' was the Hag. "She has a plan." Of course the Hag had a plan. Of course Kinny was terrified. Of course it needed moonlight. Of course, of course, of course.

It was all so obvious now. But all Kinny's warnings, the deaths, all the evidence that had mounted bit by bit over the last months, none of it had made him understand. No. Wrong. He hadn't *let* himself understand. He'd been so obsessed with Macbeth he couldn't let himself see how truly perilous the mirror was.

And Macbeth in it. Oh, Macbeth.

His chest ached with running. The shadowy countryside fell away behind him as moonlight opened the land ahead. Macbeth's land, Lucas thought, his beautiful Alba with its Goddess Ring that didn't belong in Macbeth's orderly world, though he had run to it that last grim night when there was nowhere else to go, run to it as Lucas was running, all alone, the moon-light in his eyes and darkness waiting....

The crossroads. Not a car in sight. The long abandoned railway bridge and the Stygian blackness under it. Go. It may already be too late. The laneway now. The stone circle. Four stones. More? He couldn't tell, the moonlight furred everything, but the people at least were clear. Dana, the hunchback, Kinny with hawthorn in her hair – or was that the girl with blue-black hair and hungry eyes? Lucas blinked. He was panting too hard; his eyes were playing tricks. Slow down. They'll hear you. Breathe more slowly. What was that, outside the Circle on the other side? A shadow of a person, a flash of eyes? He squinted, but now there was noth-ing. More tricks. No one else was there. Just him, and the three in the circle, and that mir-ror, that great shining silver eye with people inside it, and Dana and the hunchback holding it between them, offering it to Kinny.

"Will you take it, child?" Dana and the hunchback together, two blue-veined hands offering the mirror. "Will you be Maiden?"

"I will." A voice Lucas hardly knew, calm as a field blanketed in snow.

Lucas had let Kinny walk away. He had told her he was sick of helping her. He had been to her what they had been to Macbeth, making her rely on his help and then taking it away, and she had made that wish for him and now they were making her pay, trapped like a bear in a cage, and it was his fault, it was their fault....

"Can you repeat the Words as we have taught you?" Dana asked Kinny.

"I can."

"Then speak them. Once to awaken the Power. Once to open the way. And once, last of all, to seal."

Stop it. Have to stop it. Lucas was moving again, fast, very fast.

The calm, dead voice didn't hesitate. "Two into one. Find through this glass a past for thy future, that the name of the Goddess be not forgotten."

Faster and faster. He was running now. Light flared, brilliantly blue. Lucas charged through it. He brushed against a stone, felt the sting of nettles, ploughed on. Someone cried out; not himself; he would not listen. No time to plan. Just do it.

The hunchback was on the ground, gagging. Dana was clawing at him; then she wasn't. Kinny was shrieking. His hands were prying the mirror from her grip. "This is for you," he shouted at her. "Stop it. You'll see it's for the best. Stop."

"No, Lucas! I have to! Please —"

But he had it now. For the first time since the rehearsal hall in Stratford he held the mirror by the handle. Cool wood, scarred by an ancient burn; blue glass shimmering. Beautiful. Oh, beautiful. And the man in the glass, lined, proud; a grizzled beard, long hair parted in the middle and held in place by a narrow gold diadem, deepset blue eyes that were inward-looking and tormented.

The hunchback was getting to her feet. Dana was helping her. They were bare seconds away from responding to Lucas' attack. He was under no illusion that he could overcome them a second time. He had to do something, and he had to do it now.

Desperately he clutched the mirror. Macbeth had done something. He had said the Words that had sent the mirror far into the future. But when Macbeth had interfered in the witches' spell, the girl had already said the right spell twice. The first time awakened the Power, and the second opened the way. Kinny had said the right spell only once. If Lucas tried changing the spell to Macbeth's wording now, who knew what could happen? He couldn't risk it. He had to say the right spell first.

But he couldn't say it to the Hag.

A voice whispered in his brain. For Macbeth, then. Do it. All your life you have been waiting for this. Do it.

"Two into one," he gabbled out to that despairing face in the mirror. "Find through this glass a past for thy future, that the name of the Goddess be not forgotten."

The mirror flared blue, a second time. Quick, quick, the third time, using Macbeth's change of Words –

But he would go into the glass himself, if he said it. That was what had happened to Macbeth. If Lucas said it, he would go into the glass with Macbeth and the Hag, and they would all be prisoners in the future together.

His fingers clenched. His gaze swung desperately around the stone circle. The hunchback and Dana were joined hand to hand, and he knew they were gathering their power to attack him. And then over the ringing silence, over the dying power-line hum of the mirror's blue light, Lucas heard a voice speak out of the glass, a voice aiming straight into his own mind.

Who does this thing? Who are you, young man, to offer me your life?

Macbeth, Lucas thought joyously, his Macbeth, speaking to him at last! For a bare instant he forgot the witches, forgot the mirror in his hand, forgot everything but Macbeth. Then he was choking.

Invisible hands were strangling him...no air...and across the stone circle from him the Mother and the Maiden stood together, their fingers writing in each other's grasp, and they were staring his death at him.

"Leave him alone, Dana!" Kinny screamed. "I won't say your Words, if you hurt him. I swear I won't!"

He felt it when their stares left him. Air shuddered into his lungs. In. Out. In. Out. Spots swam before his eyes. He tried to move, but could not. He remained transfixed, holding the mirror in his right hand, his left outstretched in supplication to the witches. He could shift his eyes, but that was all. The witches had not released their hold on him.

Dana spoke then. "You will take the glass from him, Kincardine O'Neil. You will take it, and say the Words, and The Mother and I will not harm him."

Kinny moved haltingly toward him. Lucas tried to speak, but nothing came out. Despairingly, he turned his eyes back to the glass. Macbeth was still staring out at him.

I do not know you, Macbeth said to him, though his lips did not move. *Are you Alban?*

Lucas couldn't speak. But he could think. Perhaps if he thought the words very hard.... *My name is Lucas. My country — doesn't matter. You wouldn't know it.*

Not Alban, yet you offer me your life.

What did Macbeth mean? Realization hit him. That spell, offering a young body for an old soul. He'd recited it to Macbeth, because he wouldn't say it to the Hag, but he hadn't really thought about what the unaltered spell really meant.

If I took your offer, Lucas, would I be worthy of it? Would I not have become, in the moment before your death, a small and selfish man who took the life of one who had believed in him?

Lucas tried desperately to think of an answer that wouldn't be a lie.

Macbeth said sadly, *I can never accept your offer. I no longer know the truth of what I am, and I will not find it out in a world I can enter only by dishonour. But I thank you for what you would have done. I thank you mightily.*

Lucas sagged. The face of Macbeth faded. There was nothing in the mirror now but a dim arctic light. Suddenly there came a second voice. *You are a fool, Macbeth. He offers you freedom. Why do you not take it?*

I am not you, Hag. Dully. *I was a king. What is a king without his country? What am I, if Alba is gone?*

So you will not take the hope he offers?

I will not.

Then I will tell you the truth. It was I, not his generous opinion of you, that made him offer his life to you.

No, Lucas cried silently to the empty mirror. *No, I chose it. I did it on my own!*

The Hag turned on him. With horror he saw her face, puffed like a viper, venomous. *You are a fool, Lucas Cormier. Do you think anything you have done with this mirror has been of your will? It was I who made you see Macbeth and admire him and want to be him, I who had it in my mind all along that you would do what you have done here!*

The Hag took her eyes off him then, turning again to Macbeth. *In any case I would not have let him say those Words for the third time. I would have stopped him, as soon as you had agreed to allow his sacrifice. Hope offered and accepted only to be dashed to ruin along with your honour. I planned it long ago, Macbeth. Revenge for these thousand years. You have foiled it, but I will find other ways when I leave the mirror, and ways to deal with the boy.*

I'm going to die, Lucas thought. As soon as the Hag gets out of the mirror she's going to kill me. And my death won't save Kinny, it won't even save Macbeth.

He saw many things very clearly now. Kinny had been right about the mirror all along. A thousand years of Goddess Power and only the Hag to administer it, the one Sister of the Three whose role was utter destruction. And he had gone to the mirror willingly, he had chosen it! His mind flashed back to that night in Stratford, eavesdropping on Dana and the hunchback.

"She knows about the boy?"

"He's part of it."

Part of it. He'd always been part of it. And Dana had known. She had even tried to warn him. "Nothing in that mirror is worth what you will pay if you take it in your hands once more."

Lucas hated the mirror then. If he could have moved he would have smashed it against a stone, smashed it and smashed it until nothing of it was left.

All at once he saw Kinny. She had approached him from behind the looking glass and now was standing at arm's-length from it, facing him with the mirror between them. His eyes sought hers. She had warned him, and he hadn't listened to her. He'd made it harder for her every step of the way. In his obsession with the mirror he'd given the Hag the very tool they needed to trap her. Her eyes were wide, the pupils huge. He wanted to cry out to her.

And then slowly and deliberately her hand went out, reaching for the mirror.

Chapter Nineteen

Kinny knew all the arguments. she'd had them with herself, and she couldn't sort them out any more. She had wished, she had summoned Power to her bidding, and a man had died. A life for a life; her life for Alex's life. It had seemed, until now, the best that she could do.

But now everything had changed. It was impossible for her not to know what the Hag had in mind for Lucas. As soon as the spell was sealed she would kill him. And she would do it for no other reason than that she wanted to hurt Macbeth as much as possible.

She would do it in Kinny's body, twisting Kinny's hands and using Kinny's voice in a spell of destruction, and Lucas would die. And those hands and that voice would have been made hers by Kinny, given to her of her own free will when Kinny recited that spell for the third and final time. By choosing to recite it, by trying to atone for Alex's death, Kinny would be making herself responsible for Lucas' death too.

Kinny could simply refuse to say the spell. But what then? It would be only a matter of time before Dana and the hunchback found a new girl who could be persuaded to let the Hag out — and then Lucas would die anyway. Clearly, refusing to say the spell was not going to help Lucas, or anyone else.

And there was the future to consider. The hunchbacked Mother was already very old. When the Hag became Maiden and the Mother became Hag, it would not be very many years before the new Hag would need a younger body. Unless something happened to prevent it, the mirror would come into play again, with all its deadly entrapments and temptations, and some new girl would be drawn into things, and it would all begin again.

If Kinny could prevent it, and she didn't, she would be responsible for all of the things that happened afterwards. But if she actually took action to stop it, she would also become responsible for all of the things that happened thereafter. And there was only one action she could take to stop things — to do as Macbeth had done once before and send the mirror into the future. If she did that, the hunchback's mortal body would certainly never live long enough to find the mirror again. Even Dana might die before it could be found. And the Hag needed both her sisters to perform the transfer ceremony, so the death of even one of them would condemn her to stay in the mirror.

She would be stuck there, and she wouldn't be able to kill Lucas, not ever.

But if she used Macbeth's version of the spell instead of the proper one, she herself would go into the mirror as Macbeth had done. She would end up as he had ended, trapped with the Hag for eternity.

She had already faced up to the idea that her soul was going to die. It was a far worse prospect to imagine it living on like that, in never-ending hatred and despair.

It would have been easier if she could have guaranteed that the consequences would attach only to herself. But they wouldn't. Dana would lose her Sisters and her immortality; Macbeth would suffer the Hag's balked fury forever. And Kinny had too much experience of the mirror to believe that would be all. Whatever she did, she was going to cause harm. But there was Lucas standing helpless before her, her friend Lucas, waiting for her words to destroy him. That other time she had been wrong to try to help him, because he could have helped himself. Not this time.

She let her hovering hand close on the mirror in Lucas' grip. When it was hers, she turned it around. The glass faced her, faintly pulsing. The Hag became aware of her at once.

Maiden, she acknowledged. *Seal the spell. Now.*

Kinny shot a quick glance around. She was

beside a great standing stone on the perimeter of the ring, and the Mother and the Maiden were farther off, near the centre. Would it be far enough? It would have to be.

"The third time, child," Dana called. She was still crouching. There was a faint smile on her face, gentle, almost loving. "Third for the sealing."

But the Mother was standing. She stared at Kinny, and she frowned.

Kinny closed her eyes. There was no time to lose; only Dana trusted her; the hunchbacked Mother could do anything. At the moment they were using their magic to control Lucas, but that would change very quickly, once Kinny began. Hastily, but as clearly and loudly as her trembling lips allowed, Kinny started to speak.

"Two into one. Find through this glass a future for –"

Something moving, she could hear it. "– for thy past –" Speak faster.

Pain lanced through her right arm, unbearable, dizzying. She had known they would try to stop her. Ignore it. "...that the...name..."

She had to open her eyes. She had to look. There was blood everywhere. A pair of manicure scissors was sticking through her forearm. And tensed over her, smiling with horrifying politeness as she took the mirror from her nerveless hand, was Jeneva Strachan.

She was wearing one shoe only, and her caftan was split to the hip, but her elegant leather purse still hung incongruously over one shoulder. She held a tiny metal bottle open over the glass of the mirror. "I can destroy the glass," she said, evenly. "I will, if anyone here tries to stop me."

"She's bluffing," Dana said, starting forward.

"Try me," Jeneva said, and tilted the bottle.

Dana stopped so quickly she fell to one knee. The hunchback hissed with fury.

"Why, Jeneva?" Kinny clutched her dripping arm, wide-eyed with shock. "My arm...why...?"

Jeneva said, "All I wanted to do was produce my own *Macbeth* in my own way. It would have worked, too, if only *they* would have let things alone. But they had their own agenda, and they didn't let anything get in their way."

She turned toward Dana. The hand with the bottle shook. "You didn't know I knew, did you? All those things — Lucas' burn, Alex, the fire — and Joan, too, I expect, and the bus. God, the people who've been hurt by you! I watched you, I saw it all in the mirror."

"You went to the mirror?" Kinny got out, through lips twisted with pain. "The way Lucas —?"

"Not the way Lucas did!" Jeneva said contemptuously. "He went for Macbeth — yes, I saw him do it — and that was the Hag's plan, but I went of my own free will."

"You went to it because we made you aware of what it was," said the hunchback, taking a single cautious step toward Jeneva. "That very first day in your rehearsal hall, we made you see what the mirror really was. It was we who made you decide not to alter it for your play."

"You didn't make me. I chose to keep it the way it was because it showed me things. It showed me what you two were up to."

"How?" Dana asked softly, still on her knees.

"Through the Hag, how do you think? Jeneva said. The hunchbacked Mrs. Maugham took another quiet step or two forward. She was now almost even with Lucas, still standing like a statue with his empty arms out in front of him. Jeneva went on speaking. "The Hag had nothing to do but watch the outside world. She saw everything. And I saw what she saw."

"You were that close to her?" Dana's voice was insinuating.

"Don't try to make me say things I don't mean," Jeneva replied angrily. "It won't help you. I won't deny that sometimes when I looked in the mirror it seemed as if I were the one on the inside, looking out. But then I'd go away, and I'd remember. I'd remember who I was and what you three had done to me."

She raged on, not seeming to notice that the

hunchback was much closer to her than she had been. "Do you know what it is to try and try and still fail, just because someone interfered? No, you don't know, nobody's interfered with you three for a thousand years. It's about time you were reminded what it feels like."

Her fingers tightened on the mirror, and her famous actor's lungs began to project. "Find through this glass a future for thy past, that the name —"

Dana scrambled to her feet. But the hunchback was already thudding into Jeneva, knocking the bottle aside, struggling to get one hand on the mirror where the greater part of her power lay. "Give it to me. Give it —"

"— of Jeneva Strachan —"

The hunchback had a hand on it now. Her fingers tensed —

"— be not forgotten!"

There was a blinding blue flash that sent Lucas staggering into Kinny. His empty hand dropped to his side. Kinny fell down, gasping with agony as the scissors shifted in her flesh. His groping fingers felt for her, brushing her arm. She screamed.

"Kinny? Did I...? Kinny! I can't see. That light — where are you? The light blinded —"

"Here," she wept. "Here, Lucas. Oh, here."

She *was* here, not in the mirror. She was here! And the mirror was gone. She had seen it go. The mirror, and Jeneva, and the hunchback, and the Hag, gone, all gone, into the future with Macbeth.

Their fate wasn't up to her any more. She had done everything she could, and in the end, it had all been taken out of her hands.

"I didn't have to do it," Kinny said through her tears. "I didn't have to go."

He stroked her hair. "There, I can see you now, don't cry, it's all right."

"I thought it was only up to me. I thought...." She shuddered. "And it wasn't. I didn't have to do it. Jeneva did it for me."

"She didn't do it for you," a voice said wearily.

Lucas scrambled to his feet. "Dana?"

She was trudging toward them, slow, uncertain footsteps crunching through stone. With her undamaged arm Kinny wiped at her eyes. The moonlight hung heavy on the circle, dimmer now, less powerful. In it Dana looked different, an elderly stranger in a frilly dress, head hunched forward, mortal. Her round eyes shining like marbles were the only things that had not changed.

"What — happened to you?" Kinny jerked out.

"I am different, you think? I did think I might be. Time is a...strange thing." She dropped awkwardly to her knees beside Kinny, then reached for her injured arm. Kinny couldn't bring herself to move it away from her; there was something in the other woman's face that stopped her.

"Are you all right, Dana?" she whispered.

"Those scissors. Right through your arm." Her hand moved forward gently, feather-touches all along the burning. She touched the scissors lightly. "Look at me," she said to Kinny. "Trust me this one time, and do not think."

A quick pull, hard and sharp; a burst of agony, then nothing. Kinny whimpered with surprise. "It's gone," she said, with a convulsive shudder. "There's no pain at all."

"And no blood, either," Lucas said, looking wonderingly down at her arm. "You can't even see where the scissors went in." He scrutinized Dana, still kneeling heavily on the ground beside Kinny, arms slack, staring at nothing. "How did you do that? Dana?"

"A parlour trick. I seem to have one or two still. I suppose they will not disappear all at once." She smiled vaguely. "But whether I can get up or not...." She dropped forward so that she was on her hands and knees, then scrabbled in the dirt, trying to rise.

"Here," Lucas said gruffly, and bent over and took her arm, helping her to her feet. "Are your Sisters...I mean, are you alone?" he asked her with difficulty.

I will never see my sisters again." She said

wearily. "They are Three, now, anyway. They do not need me."

Kinny stared at her. "Three," she breathed.

"The Hag was already in the mirror," Dana said as if it were obvious. "The Mother and the Maiden joined her there."

"You don't mean — ! But Jeneva can't be the Maiden!" Lucas exploded. "She's *old.*"

"Not as old as I," Dana said. "Oh, no, not nearly."

"She was always a possibility, wasn't she?" Kinny said slowly, working it out as she went along. "You knew she was going to the mirror, and you didn't stop it. So you must have wanted it. And the Hag...she allowed Jeneva to see her thoughts, didn't she? It wasn't just an accident. She wanted Jeneva to be close to her."

"We needed a Maiden," Dana said simply. "You might not have...cooperated."

Lucas said angrily, "Do you use everybody?"

"Only those we need," Dana said, "and only if they allow it. Things are done if they must be done. The Goddess does not die, and her power is the power of Three, not One."

"But the mirror made Jeneva hate you! How could you ever expect her to agree to become one of you?"

"The desire for power is only one trap," Dana said. "Needs are traps. Hatred is a trap. Blaming others is a trap. People trap themselves, and then things happen. It is always the same in the end."

She closed her eyes suddenly. "But I would not have had things happen this way," she said, almost in a whisper.

Kinny put her hand on Dana's arm. "Dana?" Dana's eyes opened. All their shininess was gone. "I'm sorry," Kinny said. "Dana, I'm so sorry."

Lucas shook his head bewilderedly. "I still don't see how Jeneva can be the new Maiden. She didn't switch with the Hag, so...."

"A Maiden can be taught, given enough time," Dana said. "A mortal body could not live long enough to learn even a tenth of what is required, but in the mirror there are lifetimes and lifetimes...."

"Will Macbeth...will he have to keep on...?" Lucas stumbled to a halt.

"You gave him hope," Dana said, shrugging a little, "and you did not die because of him, and so that hope is not gone."

"The others will come out of the mirror in the end?" Kinny asked. "Jeneva and the hunchback first, I suppose, and then they'll find another girl —"

"And the Hag will become Maiden again," Dana said, "and it will all go on as it must."

"What about you, Dana?" Kinny asked. "What will you do?"

"I will grow old," she said. Again she tried to smile. "It is almost time for me to get on with that." She took a step away from them, peering a little uncertainly into the shadows.

"Where will you go?" Lucas burst out, as if he couldn't help himself.

"Not back to Edinburgh, you can be sure." This time Dana's smile was genuine. "Everett will have to replace his First Witch."

"Again," Lucas said pointedly.

Dana ignored that. "I think things will go a little better for your play now. Jeneva's 'suicide' will be splashed all over the newspapers, but that'll be the end of your media bonanza. From now on, you'll have to work for your reviews." She rubbed her forehead, then looked at Kinny. "Will you stay with the show, Kinny?"

"At least till after Edinburgh. They'll need me, now that Jeneva's —" She broke off.

"But do you *want* to stay? In the theatre, I mean?"

"I don't know," she answered with painful honesty. "I think I do a lot of things for the wrong reasons."

"So you're not going to go to theatre school?" Lucas asked.

She was silent. Until recently she had thought that great actors were great because they could impose themselves on a part and make it work. Now she knew that it was something very different. What made great acting was a self-effacing search for the truth of the character being played, and a decision to speak that truth for the character. It wasn't the Hag's kind of possession, it was more cooperative than that, but it was possession all the same.

"I'm not much good at letting other people take me over," Kinny told Lucas at last. "I seem to be better at telling them what to do, instead."

"So be a director, not an actor," Lucas said. He grinned at her wry look, then added casually, "I was thinking maybe I'd come to Montreal after the tour's over. I hear the theatre there is really worth watching."

"It is," Kinny said, "but it's mostly in French. Would you understand any of it?"

"What I've forgotten, you could translate for me. If you wanted."

Dana had listened silently, almost distantly, to their exchange.

Now she said to Lucas, as if the words came from nowhere, "You will be a great actor one day, Lucas Cormier, but you will never play Macbeth."

Lucas turned on her. "I don't need your predictions. I don't need anything from you. You were part of everything that happened, we know that, there's no point in pretending you